The Teacher's Book of Lists for Learning

Hundreds of Great Lists that Add Fascinating Facts and Fun to Every Curriculum Area

J. A. Senn

S C H O L A S T I C
PROFESSIONALBOOKS

New York • Toronto • London • Auckland • Sydney

Interior design by Robert Dominguez and Jaime Lucero for Grafica, Inc.
Cover design by Vincent Ceci and Jaime Lucero
Cover photographs by Donnelly Marks

ISBN 0-590-93100-8

Table of Contents

SOCIAL STUDIES

WORLD FACTS

LANGUAGE ARTS

READING

WRITING

MATHEMATICS

CONVERSIONS

MONEY

NUMBERS AND SYMBOLS

TIME

WEIGHTS AND MEASURES

SCIENCE

BRANCHES OF SCIENCE

ANIMALS

ECOLOGY

OUR WORLD

Introduction

Did you know that . . .

- President William Taft had a pet cow named Pauline Wayne that was allowed to graze on the White House lawn?
- there's a town in Illinois named Big Foot?
- many magazines publish writing and art by young people.
- a decillion is a number followed by 33 zeroes?
- publishing the Sunday edition of *The New York Times* newspaper consumes 10,000 trees each week?
- Donald Duck first appeared in a film in 1934?

All of these fascinating facts and many, many more are in this book: *The Teacher's Book of Lists for Learning.*

What information will you find in this book?

The lists in this book are divided mainly into different areas of study. For example in the first section, **SOCIAL STUDIES**, you will find lists about the different Presidents of the United States, their wives, and even their pets. Among the many others in this section, you will find a list that explains the amendments in the Bill of Rights, another that lists in chronological order the amazing events in the expedition of Lewis and Clark; and another that lists the achievements of the great ancient civilizations. Did you know, for instance, that back in 1100-824 B.C., the Phoenicians invented the basic alphabet that we still use today?

In **WORLD FACTS**, the next section, you will find a list that projects the growth of the world's population through the year 2025, a list that gives the origins of state names, and a really humorous list that provides the most unusual names of cities in the United States—among many others. You will even find a list of fascinating facts about the Statue of Liberty. For example, you will learn that the statue's mouth is three feet wide!

The **LANGUAGE ARTS** section is next. The first list in this section will come in handy the next time a student needs to know how to abbreviate a word or the name of a state. Included among the many other lists in this section, you will find one of commonly misspelled words and one of words that imitate sounds. There is even a list of tongue twisters. This section also has a list of magazines for young people, a list of careers for people who like to read, and a list of alternatives to written book reports—as well a list of common proofreading symbols.

Whether you teach math or not, you will find helpful, interesting lists in the **MATHEMATICS** section. Starting with a handy list of the metric system, this section also includes lists on temperature conversions from Fahrenheit to Centigrade, International forms of money, and a complete list of weights and measures.

In the **SCIENCE** section, which comes next, you will learn that a group of whales is called a *gam* or a *pod* in a list of animal names. Among the many other interesting lists in this section are the following: *Rain Forest Facts, Calories in Common Foods, Unusual Inventions, Most Common Allergies, Solar Eclipses through 2000*, and the *Coldest Cities in the U.S.*

OUR WORLD, the last section, includes lists about movies and television, music, people, sports, fads, and kids' collections. In addition, you will find in this section a list of instruments in an orchestra, a list of the most popular girls' and boys' names, a list of famous left-handed people, a list of favorite sports around the world, and a list of the origins of holidays.

How can you and your students use the information in this book?

Because of the broad appeal of this book, you should make it available to your students—either in your classroom library or through some kind of check-out system. Immediately, you and your students will find that one of the greatest uses of the information in this book is plain and simple enjoyment. You might want to encourage your students to choose a subject that interests them and then sit back and read through the lists in that section. Or tell your students to skim through the table of contents and stop and read any list that catches their curiosity. Of course, there are many other uses as well, including the following:

- as a source of ideas for a school report or project
- as the basis for charts, displays, and graphs
- as a basic reference book of general information on many subjects
- as a handy place to find answers to trivia questions
- as a convenient source of important addresses
- as a tool for practicing chronologizing, classifying, and comparing skills
- as an aid to the study of word origins and meanings, vocabulary, and spelling
- as the basis for a classroom Jeopardy™ game

After you and your students become familiar with the lists in this book, you will undoubtedly find many other uses as well. I hope you enjoy using this book as much as I enjoyed compiling it.

J. A. Senn

The Bill of Rights • Lewis and Clark • Notable First Ladies • Native American Tribes •
U.S. Presidents • Great Ancient Civilizations • Explorers of North America • The White
House • Documents in Western History • Child Rulers • The Bill of Rights • Lewis and
Clark • Notable First Ladies • Native American Tribes • U.S. Presidents • Great Ancient
Civilizations • Explorers of North America • The White House • Documents in Western
History • Child Rulers • The Bill of Rights • Lewis and Clark • Notable First Ladies •

SOCIAL STUDIES

The Presidency

THE SEQUENCE OF PRESIDENTIAL SUCCESSION

1. Vice President
2. Speaker of the House of Representatives
3. President Pro Tempore of the Senate
4. Secretary of State
5. Secretary of the Treasury
6. Secretary of Defense
7. Attorney General
8. Secretary of the Interior
9. Secretary of Agriculture
10. Secretary of Commerce
11. Secretary of Labor
12. Secretary of Heath and Human Services
13. Secretary of Housing and Urban Development
14. Secretary of Transportation
15. Secretary of Energy
16. Secretary of Education

FORMER OCCUPATIONS OF SOME PRESIDENTS

1. George Washington	surveyor, planter	8. Warren Harding	newspaper editor
2. John Adams	teacher, lawyer	9. Herbert Hoover	engineer
3. Thomas Jefferson	writer, inventor, lawyer, architect	10. Dwight Eisenhower	army general
		11. John F. Kennedy	news-paperman
4. Andrew Jackson	soldier	12. Lyndon Johnson	teacher
5. Andrew Johnson	tailor	13. Jimmy Carter	peanut farmer
6. Theodore Roosevelt	rancher	14. Ronald Reagan	actor
7. Woodrow Wilson	teacher	15. George Bush	oilman

STATISTICS OF U.S. PRESIDENTS

		party	*vice president*	*term*
1.	George Washington	none	John Adams	1789-1797
2.	John Adams	Federalist	Thomas Jefferson	1797-1801
3.	Thomas Jefferson	Dem.-Rep.	Aaron Burr	1801-1809
			George Clinton	
4.	James Madison	Dem.-Rep.	George Clinton	1809-1817
			Elbridge Gerry	
5.	James Monroe	Dem.-Rep.	Daniel D. Tompkins	1817-1825
6.	John Quincy Adams	Dem.-Rep.	John C. Calhoun	1825-1829
7.	Andrew Jackson	Democrat	John C. Calhoun	1829-1837
			Martin Van Buren	
8.	Martin Van Buren	Democrat	Richard M. Johnson	1837-1841
9.	William Henry Harrison	Whig	John Tyler	1841
10.	John Tyler	Whig	(none)	1841-1845
11.	James K. Polk	Democrat	George M. Dallas	1845-1849
12.	Zachary Taylor	Whig	Millard Fillmore	1849-1850
13.	Millard Fillmore	Whig	(none)	1850-1853
14.	Franklin Pierce	Democrat	William R. King	1853-1857
15.	James Buchanan	Democrat	John C. Breckenridge	1857-1861
16.	Abraham Lincoln	Republican	Hannibal Hamlin	1861-1865
			Andrew Jackson	
17.	Andrew Jackson	Democrat	(none)	1865-1869
18.	Ulysses S. Grant	Republican	Schuyler Colfax	1869-1877
19.	Rutherford B. Hayes	Republican	William A. Wheeler	1877-1881
20.	James A. Garfield	Republican	Chester A. Arthur	1881
21.	Chester A. Arthur	Republican	(none)	1881-1885
22.	Grover Cleveland	Democrat	Thomas A. Hendricks	1885-1889
23.	Benjamin Harrison	Republican	Levi P. Morton	1889-1893
24.	Grover Cleveland	Democrat	Adlai E. Stevenson	1893-1897
24.	William McKinley	Republican	Garret A. Hobart	1897-1901
25.	Theodore Roosevelt	Republican	Charles W. Fairbanks	1901-1909
26.	William H. Taft	Republican	James S. Sherman	1909-1913
27.	Woodrow Wilson	Democrat	Thomas R. Marshall	1913-1921
28.	Warren G. Harding	Republican	Calvin Coolidge	1921-1923
28.	Calvin Coolidge	Republican	Charles G. Dawes	1923-1929
29.	Herbert C. Hoover	Republican	Charles Curtis	1929-1933
30.	Franklin D. Roosevelt	Democrat	John Nance Garner	1933-1945
			Henry A. Wallace	
			Harry S. Truman	
31.	Harry S. Truman	Democrat	Alben W. Barkley	1945-1953
32.	Dwight D. Eisenhower	Republican	Richard M. Nixon	1953-1961
33.	John F. Kennedy	Democrat	Lyndon B. Johnson	1961-1963
34.	Lyndon B. Johnson	Democrat	Hubert Humphrey	1963-1969
35.	Richard M. Nixon	Republican	Spiro T. Agnew	1969-1974
36.	Gerald R. Ford	Republican	Nelson A. Rockefeller	1974-1977
37.	Jimmy Carter	Democrat	Walter Mondale	1977-1981
38.	Ronald Reagan	Republican	George Bush	1981-1989

ie Bill of Rights • Lewis and Clark • Notable First Ladies • Native American Tribes • U.

residents • Great Ancient Civilizations • Explorers of North America • The White

| 39. George Bush | Republican | J. Danforth Quayle | 1989-1993 |
| 40. Bill Clinton | Democrat | Albert Gore, Jr. | 1993- |

NOTABLE FIRST LADIES

1. **Abigail Smith Adams** (1744-1818): A hundred years before women were granted the right to vote, she spoke out for all women's rights—especially the right to vote and the right for equal education. She was the only first lady who also had a son who became President of the United States.

2. **Dorothea Payne Madison** (1768-1849): Called "Dolley" Madison, she was one of the most popular first ladies. During the War of 1812, she bravely stayed in the White House to protect important papers and other treasures from the advancing British troops.

3. **Lucy Ware Webb Hayes** (1831-1889): She was the first president's wife to graduate from college. She became well known for her many visits to schools, prisons, and mental institutions. Henry Wadsworth Longfellow and Oliver Wendell Holmes, two famous American poets, wrote poems to praise this exceptional woman.

4. **Frances Folsom Cleveland** (1864-1947): Because she was only 21 when she became first lady, she remains the youngest first lady. She was also the first wife of a president to give birth to a baby in the White House.

5. **Helen Herron Taft** (1861-1943): She was responsible for the planting of 3,000 cherry trees in Washington, D.C. (They were a gift to her from the mayor of Tokyo, Japan.)

6. **Anna Eleanor Roosevelt** (1884-1962): Wife of Franklin Roosevelt, she wrote a daily newspaper column, held press conferences, and served as the U.S. delegate to the United Nations. Known throughout the world, she was often called "The First Lady of the World."

7. **Jacqueline Bouvier Kennedy** (1929-1995): She supervised an historic renovation of the White House and was responsible for establishing many cultural programs at the White House.

8. **Claudia Taylor Johnson** (1912-): Known as "Lady Bird," she campaigned for a more beautiful America and lectured on ways to improve the environment. She advocated the removal of all billboards along roadsides and the planting of trees and flowers.

9. **Rosalynn Smith Carter** (1927-): She was the first president's wife to visit foreign countries on her own. She also worked hard for mental health programs and the passage of the Equal Rights Amendment.

10. **Nancy Davis Reagan** (1923-): She traveled throughout the U.S. talking to young people about her anti-drug campaign, "Say No to Drugs."

SOME PRESIDENTIAL PETS

		pet	pet's name
1.	George Washington	parrot	Polly
2.	Thomas Jefferson	mockingbird	Dick
3.	John Q. Adams	alligator	
4.	Abraham Lincoln	turkey	Jack
		goats	Nanny & Nanko
5.	Ulysses S. Grant	Newfoundland dog	Faithful
6.	Rutherford Hayes	shepherd dogs	Hector & Nellie
		English mastiff	Duke
		Siamese cat	Siam
7.	Benjamin Harrison	goat	Old Whiskers
8.	Theodore Roosevelt	garter snake	Emily Spinach
		blue macaw	Eli Yale
		small bear	Jonathan Edwards
		lizard	Bill
		hen	Baron Spreckle
		pig	Maude
		rabbit	Peter
		pony	Algonquin
		dogs	Jack, Sailor Boy, Skip & Pete
		cats	Tom Quartz & Slippers
9.	William Taft	cow	Pauline Wayne*
10.	Warren Harding	Airedale	Laddie Boy
11.	Calvin Coolidge	bobcat	Smokey
		donkey	Ebenezer
		raccoons	Horace & Rebecca
		cats	Blackie, Tiger, Bounder
		dogs	Paul Pry, Terrible Tim, Boston Beans, Peter Pan, King Kole, Bessie, Palo Alto & Rob Roy
12.	Franklin Roosevelt	Scottie dog	Fala**
13.	John F. Kennedy	parakeets	Bluebelle & Maybelle
		dogs	Charlie, Pushinka, Clipper, Wolf & Shannon
		pony	Macaroni
14.	Gerald Ford	golden retriever	Liberty
		Siamese cat	Chan
15.	Bill Clinton	cat	Socks

*The last cow to graze on the White House lawn.
**Fala was on the U.S.S. Augusta in 1941 when President Roosevelt and Winston Churchill signed the Atlantic Charter.

INTERESTING FACTS ABOUT THE WHITE HOUSE

1. Every president except George Washington has lived in the White House.

2. When John and Abigail Adams moved into the White House on November 1, 1800, there were only six rooms and an unfinished staircase. Abigail hung the laundry in the East Room and often had trouble finding enough wood for the fireplaces to keep the house warm.

3. The house was first known as the "Presidential Palace," but Jefferson changed the name to the "Executive Mansion" during his term. Although Andrew Jackson was the first to call it the *White House*, it wasn't until 1902 that the name became official when Theodore Roosevelt put it on his stationery.

4. The British burned the White House down during the War of 1812.

5. Andrew Jackson had running water first piped into the White House in 1833.

6. Millard Fillmore installed the first stove in 1850. Up until then all the cooking had been done over an open fireplace.

7. In 1877, Alexander Graham Bell personally installed one of the country's first telephones in the White House for President Rutherford Hayes.

8. President Chester Arthur had the first elevator installed in the White House in 1881; it worked only by cranking it by hand.

9. In 1891 during Benjamin Harrison's term as president, the White House became one of the first homes in the country to be wired for electricity.

10. Franklin Roosevelt finally modernized the White House kitchen by installing electric stoves and dishwashers.

United States

THE BILL OF RIGHTS*

First Amendment: guarantees freedom of religion, speech, press, assembly, and petition

Second Amendment: guarantees the right to keep and bear arms

Third Amendment: prohibits the government from taking away the homes of private citizens

Fourth Amendment: protects citizens against being searched or having their property taken away by the government without a good reason

Fifth Amendment: guarantees five rights: (1) the right to a grand jury indictment, (2) the right not to be tried twice for the same offence, (3) the right to be protected from self-incrimination, (4) the right to due process of law, and (5) the right to government compensation for the taking of private property for public use

Adopted in 1791.

Sixth Amendment: guarantees a speedy, fair jury trial

Seventh Amendment: guarantees that no judge can overrule a jury's decision except in certain instances provided by the law

Eighth Amendment: protects three rights: (1) pretrial bail should not be "excessive," (2) excessive fines are prohibited if there is a conviction, and (3) "cruel and unusual punishment" is prohibited if there is a conviction

Ninth Amendment: states that the people keep other rights not listed in the Bill of Rights

Tenth Amendment: limits the general powers of the national government in order to protect individual freedom

OTHER IMPORTANT AMENDMENTS

Thirteenth Amendment (1865): abolishes slavery in the United States

Fourteenth Amendment (1868): establishes the Bill of Rights as protection against actions by state government and guarantees equal protection under the law for all citizens

Fifteenth Amendment (1870): guarantees that a person of any race or color cannot be denied the right to vote

Ninteenth Amendment (1920): grants women the right to vote

Twenty-Second Amendment (1951): limits the President to two four-year terms in office

Twenty-Fourth Amendment (1964): outlaws the poll tax in federal elections. (A poll tax, a tax which had to be paid before someone could vote, had been used to keep African-Americans in the South from voting.)

Twenty-Fifth Amendment (1967): grants the President the power to appoint a new vice president, with the approval of Congress, if a vice president dies or leaves office in the middle of a term

Twenty-Sixth Amendment (1971): lowers the voting age to 18

NATIVE AMERICAN TRIBES

Northeast/Great Lakes Tribes	*Southeastern Tribes*	*Great Plains Tribes*
1. Delaware	1. Alabama	1. Blackfoot
2. Erie	2. Apalachee	2. Cheyenne
3. Huron	3. Calusa	3. Comanche
4. Illinois	4. Cherokee	4. Crow
5. Iroquois	5. Chickasaw	5. Iowa
6. Massachuset	6. Chippewa	6. Kansa
7. Miami	7. Choctaw	7. Missouri
8. Narraganset	8. Creek	8. Omaha
9. Shawnee	9. Natchez	9. Pueblo
10. Winnebago	10. Seminole	10. Sioux

Northwest Coast/ Plateau Tribes	California/Great Basin Tribes	Southwest Tribes
1. Cayuse	1. Cochimi	1. Apache
2. Chinook	2. Cahuilla	2. Concho
3. Flathead	3. Hupa	3. Hopi*
4. Klikitat	4. Paiute (N/S)	4. Navaho
5. Nez Perce	5. Shoshoni	5. Papago
6. Nootka	6. Ute	6. Pima
7. Palus	7. Walla Walla	7. Seri
8. Spokane	8. Washo	8. Taos*
9. Tillamook	9. Yokuts	9. Yuma
10. Yakima	10. Yuki	10. Zuni*
		*part of the Pueblo

A TIME LINE OF THE AMERICAN REVOLUTION

Feb. 9, 1775: The British Parliament declares that Massachusetts is in revolt against the crown.

March 23, 1775: Patrick Henry delivers his "Give me liberty or give me death" speech before the provincial Congress.

April 18, 1775: Paul Revere rides out to warn the Minutemen of the coming British raid on Concord.

April 19, 1775: Lexington and Concord, MA, are the sites of the first skirmishes between colonial Minutemen and British soldiers. The colonial siege on Boston begins soon after.

May 10-12, 1775: Colonial troops seize Fort Ticonderoga and Crown Point.

May 31, 1775: The Continental Army is organized from colonial troops in the Boston area.

June 15, 1775: George Washington becomes the commander of the new Continental Army.

June 17, 1775: The Battle of Bunker Hill, the first major battle of the war, takes place.

October 1775: The Second Continental Congress creates the American Navy.

Feb. 1776: The British suffer defeat at Moore's Creek Bridge in the Carolinas.

July 4, 1776: The Second Continental Congress proclaims its Declaration of Independence.

Aug. 27, 1776: British force the American withdrawal from New York, across New Jersey, to Pennsylvania.

Oct. 28, 1776: Washington's troops retreat after the Battle of White Plains.

Nov. 16-20, 1776: The British take Fort Washington and Fort Lee.

Dec. 25, 1776: Washington crosses the Delaware River, capturing over 900 Hessians in a raid at Trenton.

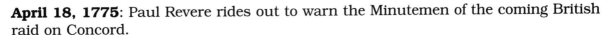

Aug. 16, 1777: The Americans defeat the British at Bennington, Vermont.

Sept. 26, 1777: The British occupy Philadelphia, Pennsylvania, following their victory at Brandywine Creek.

Oct. 4, 1777: After a failed attack on Germantown, Washington and his troops make their winter quarters in Valley Forge.

Oct. 17, 1777: After several major British defeats and the surrender of 5,700 British troops, the tide of the war turns in the Americans' favor.

Nov. 15, 1777: Congress adopts the Articles of Confederation. (They are later ratified in 1781.)

Feb. 6, 1778: With the help of French soldier Marquis de Lafayette, the Americans sign a formal alliance with France.

June 1778: The British abandon Philadelphia and withdraw to New York City as a French fleet approaches American waters.

Dec. 28, 1778: The British take Savannah, Georgia.

Jan. 29, 1779: The British take Augusta, Georgia, and keep their stronghold in the South.

June 1779: Joining the war on the American side, Spain hopes to regain Florida and Gibraltar.

Sept. 23, 1779: Captain John Paul Jones, commander of the *Bonhomme Richard*, is victorious over *Serapis* in British waters.

May 12, 1780: The British take Charleston, North Carolina, capturing 5,400 American troops.

Sept. 25, 1780: American General Benedict Arnold joins the British after his treason is discovered.

Oct. 7, 1780: The Americans get their first southern victory at Kings Mountain.

Jan. 1781: Mutinies by American troops in Pennsylvania and New Jersey are quashed.

Jan. 17, 1781: The Americans win the Battle of Cowpens in the South.

March 15, 1781: The Americans win the Battle of Guilford Court House, an important victory, and then force British General Charles Cornwallis to withdraw to Wilmington.

Aug. 1, 1781: A 7,500-strong British force conducts raids on Virginia and forces the Americans back to Yorktown.

Aug. 1781: The siege of Yorktown, the last battle of the war, begins. The French fleet drives off the British Navy, isolating the British at Yorktown. Together the Americans and the French surround the British.

Oct. 19, 1781: Cornwallis and his troops are forced to surrender.

Feb. 27, 1782: The British Parliament orders an end to any further fighting. Prime Minister Lord Frederick North is thrown out, and the British troops in America retreat to New York City.

Sept. 3, 1783 : The Treaty of Paris is signed.

Nov. 25, 1783: The British troops are withdrawn to England.

A TIME LINE OF THE LEWIS AND CLARK EXPEDITION

April 30, 1803: The United States buys Louisiana, the land between the Mississippi River and the Rocky Mountains, from France for $15 million.

May 14, 1804: With a commission from President Thomas Jefferson, Meriwether Lewis and William Clark—along with a 30-man expedition—leave St. Louis to explore the land acquired in the Louisiana Purchase, study the plant and animal life, and make friends with the Indians.

May 25, 1804: The expedition passes the last frontier settlement.

Aug. 25, 1804: The first Indian council is held in what is now Council Bluffs, Iowa. Lewis and Clark promise the Indians U.S. protection.

Oct. 26, 1804: The expedition establishes Ft. Mandan in what is now South Dakota and spends the winter there. Sacajawea and her French-Canadian husband join the expedition. Sacajawea gives birth to a baby boy.

April 5, 1805: The expedition continues north up the Missouri River, and a party is sent back to St. Louis with letters and trinkets for the President.

June 15, 1805: The Great Falls of the Missouri River is reached. It takes one month to carry the canoes 18 miles around the falls.

Aug. 12, 1805: After reaching the source the Missouri River, the expedition encounters Shoshone Indians. Sacajawea, who is a Shoshone, gains the Indians' trust.

Aug. 1805: The expedition begins its 300-mile overland journey.

Nov. 5, 1805: Clark writes that they can see the Pacific Ocean.

Nov. 1805–March 1806: The expedition builds Fort Clatsop along the Pacific, and Lewis and Clark map their entire journey.

March 23, 1806: The return journey begins.

Sept. 23, 1806: The expedition returns to St. Louis, ending its 6,000-mile exploration.

1806: Lewis is named governor of the Louisiana Territory, and Clark is named general of militia and Indian agent.

1814: Lewis and Clark's *History of the Expedition* is published.

1905: The complete journals of Lewis and Clark's expedition are published.

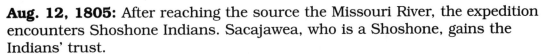

A TIME LINE OF CIVIL RIGHTS IN THE 20TH CENTURY U.S.

1941: President Franklin D. Roosevelt outlaws discrimination in employment in the defense industry.

1942: The Congress of Racial Equality (CORE) is formed to work for black equality.

1946: President Harry S. Truman's Committee on Civil Rights suggests 27 civil rights acts to end discrimination; none is enacted.

1947: CORE stages its first freedom ride to challenge segregation on interstate transit.

1948: President Truman desegregates the armed forces.

1954: In the case *Brown v. Board of Education of Topeka, Kansas,* the Supreme Court declares that "separate but equal" schools for black and white children are unconstitutional.

1955: Rosa Parks, a black resident of Montgomery, Alabama, is arrested for refusing to move to the back of a city bus.

1957: Martin Luther King, Jr. organizes a bus boycott in Montgomery that eventually forces the bus company to accept desegregation.

1957: Congress passes the Civil Rights Act to study racial conditions in the U.S.

1957: Martin Luther King, Jr. creates the Southern Christian Leadership Conference (SCLC) that uses nonviolent means to protest discrimination.

1960: The Student Nonviolent Coordinating Committee (SNCC) forms during lunch-counter sit-ins in Greensboro, North Carolina. The members support militant nonviolent action instead of nonaggressive nonviolence.

1962: The Council of Federated Organizations forms to register black voters.

1962: Federal troops protect the right of James Meredith, a black student, to enroll at the University of Mississippi. The troops remain at the school until Meredith graduates the following year.

1963: In Detroit, 200,000 people march for racial equality.

1963: Protests in Birmingham, Alabama, in April and May get national media attention because police use fire hoses and dogs to break up demonstrations.

1963: Medgar Evers, a field secretary for the NAACP, is shot and killed.

1963: A crowd of 250,000 participate in the March on Washington in August.

1964: Congress passes the Civil Rights Act of 1964 that bans all discrimination in public places, creates the Equal Employment Opportunity Commission, and guarantees equal voting rights for blacks.

1964: The 24th Amendment to the Constitution, which outlaws poll taxes, is ratified.

1964: Martin Luther King, Jr., is awarded the Nobel Peace Prize.

1964: Three young civil rights workers, Michael Schwerner, Andrew Goodman, and James Chaney, are murdered in Mississippi because they were registering black voters.

1965: A march for black voting rights is stopped in Selma, Alabama, because of violence.

1965: Congress passes the Voting Rights Act, which outlaws tests that were used to prevent black people from registering to vote.

1965: In August, 34 die and $35 million in property damage occurs in riots in the Watts section of Los Angeles.

1966: In Chicago, 4,200 National Guardsmen are used to stop race riots.

1967: In the first 9 months of 1967, a total of 164 riots break out throughout the U.S.

1967: President Lyndon Johnson's National Advisory Committee finds that racism is the main cause of all of the recent riots.

1968: Martin Luther King, Jr., is killed in Memphis, Tennessee, on April 4. Mass riots break out in more than 40 cities. Rev. Ralph Abernathy takes over the presidency of the SCLC.

1968: Congress passes the Civil Rights Act of 1968 that outlaws housing discrimination and harassment of civil-rights workers.

1969: The Congressional Black Caucus forms.

1972: Congress passes the Equal Employment Opportunity Act that allows for the special hiring and promotion of women and minorities.

AMERICAN INVOLVEMENT IN WARS

1. American Revolution 1775-1781
2. War of 1812 1812-1815
3. Mexican War 1846-1848
4. Civil War 1861-1865
5. Spanish-American War 1898
6. World War I 1917-1918
7. World War II 1941-1845
8. Korean War 1950-1953
9. Vietnam War 1957-1975
10. Persian Gulf War 1990-1991

EXCEPTIONAL 20TH CENTURY AMERICAN WOMEN

1. **Maya Angelou**, (1928–), writer, poet
2. **Elizabeth Arden**, (1878–1966), leader in the cosmetics industry
3. **Ethel Barrymore**, (1879–1959), actress
4. **Gwendolyn Brooks**, (1917–), writer and first black woman to win a Pulitzer Prize for poetry
5. **Pearl S. Buck**, (1892–1973), writer and first woman to win the Nobel Prize for literature
6. **Rachel Carson**, (1907–1964), writer and environmentalist
7. **Ella C. Deloria**, (1888–1971), a Dakota Sioux who devoted her life to the study and preservation of Native American culture

8. **Geraldine Ferraro**, (1935–), first woman to be nominated for vice president of the U.S. by a major political party

9. **Ella Fitzgerald**, (1918–1996), jazz and popular singer

10. **Peggy Fleming**, (1948–), world champion figure skater

11. **Dian Fossey**, (1932–1985), conservationist and gorilla researcher

12. **Katharine Hepburn**, (1909–), actress and two–time winner of the Oscar

13. **Zora Neal Hurston**, (1901–1960), Black folklorist, writer and anthropologist

14. **Florence Griffith Joyner**, (1959–), track and field champion

15. **Coretta Scott King**, (1927–), champion of civil rights

16. **Clare Booth Luce**, (1903–), writer and first woman to serve as a U.S. ambassador to a foreign country

17. **Aimee Semple McPherson**, (1890–1944), religious leader

18. **Margaret Mead**, (1901–1978), anthropologist and writer

19. **Edna St. Vincent Millay**, (1892–1950), poet and writer

20. **Sandra Day O'Connor**, (1930–), first woman named as an associate justice for the U. S. Supreme Court in 1981

21. **Georgia O'Keeffe**, (1887–1986), artist

22. **Frances Perkins**, (1880–1965), first woman cabinet member in U.S. history

23. **Leontyne Price**, (1927–), Black soprano who gave 118 performances at the Metropolitan Opera House

24. **Amelia Earhart Putnam**, (1897–1937), first women to pilot a plane across the Atlantic

25. **Janet Rankin**, (1880–1973), first woman to be elected to the U.S. House of Representatives

26. **Sally Ride**, (1951–), first American woman astronaut

27. **Eleanor Roosevelt**, (1884–1962), political activist and U.S. delegate to the United Nations

28. **Wilma Rudolph**, (1940–), first woman to win three gold medals in the Olympics

29. **Gloria Steinem**, (1934–), feminist and founder of *Ms.* magazine in 1972

30. **Rosalyn S. Yalow**, (1921–), physicist and medical researcher

A TIME LINE OF WOMEN'S RIGHTS IN THE U.S.

1777: Abigail Adams writes to her husband, John Adams, that women "will not hold ourselves bound by any laws in which we have no voice."

1833: Oberlin becomes the first U.S. coeducational college.

1841: A college degree is finally given to a woman.

1848: Lucretia Mott and Elizabeth Cady Stanton hold the first women's rights convention at Seneca Falls, New York, on July 19-20.

1848: New York passes a law that allows married women to own real estate.

1849: Female doctors are allowed to practice in the U.S.

1850: The first national Women's Rights Convention is held in Worcester, Massachusetts.

1869: Susan B. Anthony and Elizabeth Stanton begin the National Women's Suffrage Association.

1869: Wyoming Territory gives women the vote. It also becomes the first state to do so when it is admitted to the Union in 1890.

1869: Female lawyers are licensed in the U.S.

1878: A U.S. Constitutional amendment to grant full suffrage to women is introduced in Congress but is defeated. (It is introduced again every year until it finally passes in 1920.)

1920: The 19th Amendment to the U.S. Constitution guarantees women the right to vote.

1964: The U.S. Civil Rights Act of 1964 forbids discrimination on the basis of sex, race, religion, or national origin.

1975: The U.S. Equal Credit Opportunity Act forbids discrimination against women when granting loans and credit.

World

FORMS OF GOVERNMENTS

definition

1. emirate — a country ruled by an emir, a native prince, Chieftan, or governor; for example, Kuwait is an emirate

2. monarchy — a country ruled by a king or queen because of heredity; for example, Saudi Arabia

3. principality — a country ruled by a prince; for example, Monaco

4. republic — a country governed by a president (or similar leader) and majority rule; for example, France and the United States

5. sultanate — a country ruled by a sultan, a king of a Muslim state; for example, Oman

he Bill of Rights • Lewis and Clark • Notable First Ladies • Native American Tribes • U
residents • Great Ancient Civilizations • Explorers of North America • The White

PERIODS OF WORLD HISTORY

1.	the Stone Age	2,000,000 B.C. – 8,000 B.C.
2.	the New Stone Age	8000 B.C. – 3500 B.C.
3.	the Rise of Civilization	3500 B.C. – 2000 B.C.
4.	Classical Civilization	2000 B.C. – A.D. 476
5.	the Middle Ages	450 – 1300
6.	the Renaissance and Exploration	1300 – 1650
7.	European Enlightenment and Revolution	1650 – 1850
8.	the Age of Imperialism	1850 – 1914
9.	World Wars	1914 – 1945
10.	the Modern World	1945 – Present

IMPORTANT DOCUMENTS IN WESTERN HISTORY

313 A.D.   **Edict of Milan**: Romans grant religious freedom to Christians.

1215   **Magna Carta**: King John guarantees basic rights, such as trial by jury, and lays the foundation for English law.

1517   **95 Theses**: Martin Luther begins the Protestant Reformation.

1776   **U.S. Declaration of Independence**: The Second Continental Congress declares the colonies independent of Great Britain.

1787   **U.S. Constitution**: It establishes a democratic form of government.

1789   **Declaration of the Rights of Man and of the Citizen**: French National Assembly declares an individual's right to representation and equality, and the freedom of press, speech, and religion.

1791   **U.S. Bill of Rights**: The Amendments to the U.S. Constitution guarantee freedom of speech, religion, press, and other basic human rights.

1804   **Code Napoleon**: Napoleon Bonaparte establishes the basis of modern civil law.

1848   *Communist Manifesto*: Karl Marx and Friedrich Engels call for a revolution by workers.

1861   **Edict of Emancipation**: Russian Czar Alexander II frees millions of serfs.

1862   **Emancipation Proclamation**: Abraham Lincoln declares freedom for slaves in the Confederacy.

1918   **Fourteen Points**: U.S. President Woodrow Wilson's plan for world peace leads to the formation of the League of Nations.

1925   *Mein Kampf*: Adolf Hitler details his plans for German control of the world.

1941   **Atlantic Charter**: President Franklin Roosevelt and British Prime Minister Winston Churchill's detailed policy for world peace becomes the basis for the United Nations Charter.

1945   **United Nations Charter**: This document creates the United Nations.

1947   **Truman Doctrine**: U.S. President Harry Truman calls for a stop to the spread of communism.

1948   **Universal Declaration of Human Rights**: UN General Assembly declares basic human rights for all people.

1972   **Plaque on the *Pioneer 10* space probe**: It attempts to communicate with life beyond this solar system.

GREAT ANCIENT CIVILIZATIONS

		dates	achievements
1.	**Sumerians** lived in what is now Iraq	3500 B.C. – 2000 B.C.	first people to develop word–writing—wrote on clay tablets
2.	**Egyptians** lived along the Nile River	3100 B.C. – 525 B.C.	built huge temples and pyramids out of stone; invented writing called *hiero-glyphics*
3.	**Minoans** lived on the island of Crete near Greece	3000 B.C. – 1100 B.C.	made brightly patterned pottery and wall paintings; built large outdoor theaters and loved to watch sporting events
4.	**Babylonians** lived in what is now Iraq	1900 B.C. – 538 B.C.	great lawmakers, scientists and mathematicians; first people to count seconds and minutes by 60s
5.	**Phoenicians** lived on the eastern coast of the Mediterranean	1100 B.C. – 842 B.C.	invented an alphabet that was improved by the Greeks and is still used in the West today; skillful cloth makers, world traders, and sailors
6.	**Hebrews** lived at various times in what is now Israel and Jordan	from 1000 B.C. – 587 B.C.	various Hebrews wrote the books of the Old Testament of the Bible; King Solomon, a well known king of Israel, built a great temple in Jerusalem
7.	**Assyrians** lived in what is now Iraq	800 B.C. – 612 B.C.	formed the first great army with iron weapons; as a result, they were great warriors
8.	**Greeks** lived in the southern part of what is now Greece	from 800 B.C. – 197 B.C.	created the first democractic government; built great buildings and sculptures; and had many wise scientists and philosophers
9.	**Persians** lived in an area from the Indus River to the Aegean Sea at the height of their empire	700 B.C. – 331 B.C.	built huge palaces of mud, brick, and stone; had a system of mail delivery; legendary beasts appeared in their wall paintings and sculptures
10.	**Romans** controlled all the lands around the Mediterranean at the peak of their power	735 B.C. – 476 A.D.	first to control a vast area from a central place while allowing cities some autonomy; used their army to build bridges and roads and to improve the material lives of conquered people

CHILD RULERS

	lived	ages ruled
1. Tutankhamen, Pharaoh of Ancient Egypt	c. 1358 B.C.–?	8 – ?
2. Edward V, King of England	1438 – ?	13 – ?
3. Edward VI, King of England	1547 – 1553	10 – 16

4. Francis II, King of France	1559 – 1560	15 – 16
5. Peter I, Ruler of Russia	1682 – 1725	10 – 53

WORLD'S LONGEST REIGNING MONARCHS

	age of accession	reign	number of years
1. Louis XIV of France	5	1643–1715	72
2. John II of Liechtenstein	18	1858–1929	71
3. Franz-Josef of Austria–Hungary	18	1848–1916	67
4. Victoria of United Kingdom	18	1837–1901	63
5. Hirohito of Japan	25	1926–1989	62
6. George III of United Kingdom	22	1760–1820	59
7. Louis XV of France	5	1715–1774	59
8. Pedro II of Brazil	6	1831–1889	58
9. Wilhelmina of Netherlands	10	1890–1948	58
10. Henry III of England	9	1216–1272	56

FAMOUS EXPLORERS OF NORTH AMERICA

	date	explorer	nationality	discovery or area explored
1.	1492–93	Chistopher Columbus	Italian	Bahamas, Cuba, Hispaniola
2.	1513	Juan Ponce de Leon	Spanish	Florida
3.	1539–41	Hernando de Soto	Spanish	mouth of Mississippi River
4.	1540	Garcia Lopez de Cardenas	Spanish	Grand Canyon/Colorado River
5.	1540	Francisco V. de Coronado	Spanish	Southwestern U.S.
6.	1577–80	Sir Francis Drake	English	California coast
7.	1607	Capt. John Smith	English	Atlantic coast
8.	1609–10	Henry Hudson	Eng./Dutch	Hudson River/Hudson Bay
9.	1634	Jean Nicolet	French	Lake Michigan/Wisconsin
10.	1789	David Thompson	Canadian	Western Canada

FIRST COUNTRIES TO ALLOW WOMEN TO VOTE

country	year	country	year
1. New Zealand	1893	8. Canada	1918
2. Australia	1902	9. Germany	1918
3. Finland	1906	10. Great Britian	1918
4. Norway	1907	11. Poland	1918
5. Netherlands	1917	12. Denmark	1918
6. USSR	1917	13. United States	1920
7. Austria	1918		

Origins of State Names • Most Populated Cities • Largest Deserts • Famous World Structu
Largest Countries in the World • Oceans • Important U.S. Addresses • The Statue of Libe
Longest Rivers • Amusement Parks in the U.S. • Origins of State Names • Most Popula
ities • Largest Deserts • Famous World Structu Largest Countries in the World • Ocea
Important U.S. Addresses • The Statue of Liberty • Longest Rivers • Amusement Parks
e U.S. • Origins of State Names • Most Populated Cities • Largest Deserts • Famous Wo

WORLD FACTS

Language

MOST WIDELY SPOKEN LANGUAGES THROUGHOUT THE WORLD

language	spoken by
1. Chinese	more than 1 billion people (The principal dialect is Mandarin.)
2. English	300–400 million people (As many as one-third of the people in the world are able to speak English.)
3. Hindi	250–300 million people (Hindi and English are the two official languages of India.)
4. Russian	about 250–300 million people
5. Malay	180 million people—including variants and dialects of Malay (It is the official language of Indonesia.)
6. Arabic	at least 165 million people (It is the official language in 18 countries in N. Africa and the Middle East. It is also the language of the *Koran*, the holy book of the Muslims.)
7. Bengali	150 million people (It is the official language of Bangladesh.)
8. Spanish	125–320 million people worldwide (It is the official language of 20 nations, territories, and colonies.)
9. Japanese	more than 125 million people
10. Portuguese	100–170 million people (It is spoken by almost everyone in Brazil, but it is also the official language in 6 other countries, mostly in southern Africa.)
11. French	100–150 million people (It is the official language of 37 countries, colonies, and territories in Europe, Africa, the Americas, and the Pacific.
12. German	90–150 million people (It is the official language of 6 European countries, including Germany, Austria, Switzerland, Luxembourg, Liechtenstein, and Belgium.)
13. Urdu	50–90 million people (It is the official language of Pakistan, but many people in India also speak Urdu.)

MOST STUDIED LANGUAGES IN U.S. COLLEGES

1. Spanish
2. French
3. German
4. Italian
5. Japanese
6. Russian
7. Latin
8. Chinese
9. Ancient Greek
10. Hebrew

LANGUAGES SPOKEN MOST OFTEN IN THE U.S.

1. English
2. Spanish
3. French
4. German
5. Italian
6. Chinese
7. Tagalog
8. Polish
9. Korean
10. Vietnamese

Population

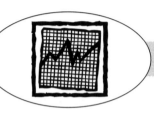

GROWTH OF THE WORLD'S POPULATION

	year	estimated total
1.	1000	254,000,000
2.	1500	460,000,000
3.	1700	679,000,000
4.	1800	954,000,000
5.	1900	1,633,000,000
6.	1950	2,515,312,000
7.	1960	3,019,376,000
8.	1970	3,697,918,000
9.	1980	4,450,210,000
10.	1993	5,554,552,000

PROJECTED GROWTH OF THE WORLD'S POPULATION

	year	highest estimate
1.	2000	6,410,707,000
2.	2010	7,561,301,000
3.	2015	8,167,357,000
4.	2020	8,791,432,000
5.	2025	9,422,749,000

MOST HIGHLY POPULATED CITIES IN THE UNITED STATES

	total in 1990*
1. New York City, New York	7,322,564
2. Los Angeles, California	3,485,398
3. Chicago, Illinois	2,783,726
4. Philadelphia, Pennsylvania	1,585,577
5. San Diego, California	1,110,549
6. Miami, Florida	3,471,000
7. Detroit, Michigan	1,027,974

According to the U.S. Bureau of the Census

MOST POPULATED CITIES IN THE U.S. IN 1900 AND THEIR RANK IN THE 1990 CENSUS

1900 rank	1900 population	city and state	1990 rank	1990 population
1.	3,437,202	New York, New York	(1)	7,322,564
2.	1,698,575	Chicago, Illinois	(3)	2,783,726
3.	1,293,697	Philadelphia, Pennsylvania	(5)	1,585,577
4.	575,238	St. Louis, Missouri	(34)	396,685
5.	560,892	Boston, Massachusetts	(20)	574,283
6.	508,957	Baltimore, Maryland	(13)	736,014
7.	381,768	Cleveland, Ohio	(24)	505,616
8.	352,387	Buffalo, New York	(50)	328,123
9.	342,782	San Francisco, California	(14)	723,959
10.	325,902	Cincinnati, Ohio	(45)	364,040

United States Geography

REGIONS OF THE U.S. MAINLAND*

	includes
1. New England	CT, ME, MA, NH, RI, VT
2. Middle Atlantic	NJ, NY, PA
3. Southeast	AL, AR, DE, FL, GA, KY, LA, MD, MS, NC, SC, TN, VA, WV
4. Midwest	IL, IN, IA, KS, MI, MN, MO, NE, ND, OH, SD, WI
5. Rocky Mountain	CO, ID, MT, NV, UT, WY
6. Southwest	AZ, NM, OK, TX
7. Pacific Coast	CA, OR, WA

For the meaning of state abbrieviations, see page 42.

IMPORTANT FACTS ABOUT THE UNITED STATES

1. land   3,536,278 square miles
2. water   251,041 square miles
3. elevation   highest: Mt. McKinley, (Denali) Alaska—20,320 feet (6,194 m.) above sea level
   lowest: Death Valley, California—282 feet (86 m.) below sea level
4. northernmost city   Barrow, Alaska
5. southernmost city   Hilo, Hawaii
6. easternmost city   Eastport, Maine
7. westernmost city   Atka, Alaska
8. population (1994)   260,341,000
9. capital   Washington, D.C.
10. form of government   republic
11. flag   red, white, and blue and a star for each state, adopted on June 14, 1777
12. bird   bald eagle, adopted on June 20, 1782
13. flower   rose, adopted on October 7, 1986
14. motto   "In God We Trust," adopted on July 30, 1956
15. national anthem   "The Star-Spangled Banner," adopted on March 3, 1931

SOME MAJOR U.S. EXPORTS AND IMPORTS*

exports	value
1. electrical machinery	$44.3 billion
2. cars, trucks, and parts	41.1 billion
3. computers and office machinery	30.9 billion
4. airplanes and parts	28.7 billion
5. general industrial machinery	21.8 billion

imports	value
1. cars, trucks, and parts	$91.0 billion
2. electrical machinery	57.7 billion
3. computer and office machinery	52.1 billion
4. crude oil	38.5 billion
5. clothing	36.7 billion

In 1994, the total value of all U.S. exports was $512.7 billion, and the total value of all imports was $663.8 billion.

STATISTICS OF THE 50 STATES

	capital	population in 1990	rank today	entered union	order of entry into union
1. Alabama	Montgomery	4,040,587	22	12/14/1819	22
2. Alaska	Juneau	550,043	49	1/3/19/59	49
3. Arizona	Phoenix	3,665,228	24	2/14/1912	48
4. Arkansas	Little Rock	2,350,725	33	6/15/1836	25

state	capital	population in 1990	rank today	entered union	order of entry into union
5. California	Sacramento	29,760,021	1	9/9/1850	31
6. Colorado	Denver	3,294,394	26	8/1/1876	38
7. Connecticut	Hartford	3,287,116	27	1/9/1788	5
8. Delaware	Dover	666,168	46	12/7/1787	1
9. Florida	Tallahassee	12,937,926	4	3/3/1845	27
10. Georgia	Atlanta	6,478,216	11	1/2/1788	4
11. Hawaii	Honolulu	1,108,229	40	8/21/1959	50
12. Idaho	Boise	1,006,749	42	7/3/1890	43
13. Illinois	Springfield	11,430,602	6	12/3/1818	21
14. Indiana	Indianapolis	5,544,159	14	12/11/1816	19
15. Iowa	Des Moines	2,776,755	30	12/28/1846	29
16. Kansas	Topeka	2,477,574	32	1/29/1861	34
17. Kentucky	Frankfort	3,685,296	23	6/1/1792	15
18. Louisiana	Baton Rouge	4,219,973	21	4/30/1812	18
19. Maine	Augusta	1,227,928	38	3/15/1820	23
20. Maryland	Annapolis	4,781,468	19	4/28/1788	7
21. Massachusetts	Boston	6,016,425	13	2/6/1788	6
22. Michigan	Lansing	9,295,297	8	1/26/1837	26
23. Minnesota	St. Paul	4,375,099	20	5/11/1858	32
24. Mississippi	Jackson	2,573,216	31	12/10/1817	20
25. Missouri	Jefferson City	5,117,073	15	8/10/1821	24
26. Montana	Helena	799,065	44	11/8/1889	41
27. Nebraska	Lincoln	1,578,385	36	3/1/1867	37
28. Nevada	Carson City	1,201,833	39	10/31/1864	36
29. New Hampshire	Concord	1,109,252	41	6/21/1788	9
30. New Jersey	Trenton	7,730,188	9	12/18/1787	3
31. New Mexico	Santa Fe	1,515,069	37	1/6/1912	47
32. New York	Albany	17,990,455	2	7/26/1788	11
33. North Carolina	Raleigh	6,628,637	10	11/21/1789	12
34. North Dakota	Bismarck	638,800	47	11/2/1889	39
35. Ohio	Columbus	10,847,115	7	3/1/1803	17
36. Oklahoma	Oklahoma City	3,145,585	28	11/16/1907	46
37. Oregon	Salem	2,842,321	29	2/14/1859	33
38. Pennsylvania	Harrisburg	11,881,643	5	12/12/1787	2
39. Rhode Island	Providence	1,003,464	43	5/29/1790	13
40. South Carolina	Columbia	3,486,703	25	5/23/1788	8
41. South Dakota	Pierre	696,004	45	2/2/1889	40
42. Tennessee	Nashville	4,877,185	17	6/1/1796	16
43. Texas	Austin	16,986,510	3	12/29/1845	28
44. Utah	Salt Lake City	1,722,850	35	1/4/1896	45
45. Vermont	Montpelier	562,758	48	3/4/1791	14
46. Virginia	Richmond	6,187,358	12	6/25/1788	10
47. Washington	Olympia	4,866,692	18	11/11/1889	42
48. West Virginia	Charleston	1,793,477	34	6/20/1863	35
49. Wisconsin	Madison	4,891,769	16	5/29/1848	30
50. Wyoming	Cheyenne	453,588	50	7/10/1890	44

ORIGINS OF STATE NAMES

		origin
1.	Alabama	from a tribe of the Creek confederacy
2.	Alaska	Russian version of Aleut word meaning "great land"
3.	Arizona	Spanish version of Pima word meaning "little spring place"
4.	Arkansas	French version of *Kansas*, a Sioux word meaning "south wind people"
5.	California	mythical island paradise in Spanish literature; from *calo forno*, meaning "hot oven" in Spanish
6.	Colorado	Spanish word for "red"
7.	Connecticut	Algonquin word meaning "beside the long river"
8.	Delaware	honors Lord De La Warr, an early governor of Virginia
9.	Florida	Spanish word meaning "feast of flowers"
10.	Georgia	honors King George II of England
11.	Hawaii	Polynesian word for "homeland"
12.	Idaho	Shoshoni word for "salmon tribe" or "light on the mountains"
13.	Illinois	Algonquin word meaning "men" or "warriors"
14.	Indiana	means "land of the Indians"
15.	Iowa	Sioux word meaning "beautiful land"
16.	Kansas	Sioux word meaning "south wind people"
17.	Kentucky	Iroquois word meaning "meadowland"
18.	Louisiana	honors Louis XIV of France
19.	Maine	from "The Main," used to distinguish the mainland from the offshore islands
20.	Maryland	honors Queen Henrietta Marie
21.	Massachusetts	Algonquin word meaning "large mountain place"
22.	Michigan	Chippewa word for "great water"
23.	Minnesota	Sioux word for "sky-tinted water"
24.	Mississippi	Chippewa word for "great river"
25.	Missouri	named after the Missouri Indian tribe (*Missouri* means "town of large canoes")
26.	Montana	Spanish word meaning "mountains"
27.	Nebraska	Omaha name for Platte River, which means "broad river"
28.	Nevada	Spanish word meaning "snow-clad"
29.	New Hampshire	named for the English county of Hampshire
30.	New Jersey	named for the island of Jersey in the English Channel
31.	New Mexico	named for the Aztec war god Mexitil
32.	New York	honors an Englishman, the Duke of York
33.	N. Carolina	honors King Charles I of England
34.	N. Dakota	Sioux word meaning "friend" or "ally"
35.	Ohio	Iroquois word for "beautiful river"
36.	Oklahoma	Choctaw word meaning "red people"
37.	Oregon	Native American word meaning "beautiful water"
38.	Pennsylvania	honors Admiral William Penn, the father of the founder of the colony
39.	Rhode Island	named for the Greek island of Rhodes
40.	S. Carolina	honors King Charles I of England
41.	S. Dakota	Sioux word meaning "friend" or "ally"
42.	Tennessee	named after the Cherokee villages on the Little Tennessee River

43.	Texas	Caddo word meaning "friendly tribe"
44.	Utah	refers to the Ute tribe, meaning "people of the mountains"
45.	Vermont	from the French words for "green mountain"
46.	Virginia	honors "Virgin Queen" Elizabeth I of England
47.	Washington	honors George Washington, the first President of the U.S.
48.	West Virginia	honors "Virgin Queen" Elizabeth I of England
49.	Wisconsin	Chippewa word meaning "grassy place"
50.	Wyoming	a Delaware Indian word meaning "mountains and valleys alternating"

MOST COMMON U.S. CITY NAMES

1.	Fairview	66	6.	Centerville	39
2.	Midway	52	7.	Mount Pleasant	38
3.	Oak Grove	44	8.	Georgetown	37
4.	Franklin	40	9.	Salem	36
5.	Riverside	40	10.	Greenwood	34

MOST UNUSUAL U.S. CITY NAMES

1. Acres of Diamonds, Florida
2. Big Foot, Illinois
3. Ding Dong, Texas
4. Do Stop, Kentucky
5. Eek, Alaska
6. Frankenstein, Missouri
7. Gun Barrel City, Texas
8. King Arthur's Court, Michigan
9. Lollipop, Texas
10. Muck City, Alabama
11. Odd, West Virginia
12. Okay, Oklahoma
13. Sandwich, Illinois
14. Snowball, Alaska
15. Sweet Lips, Tennessee
16. Two Egg, Florida
17. Uncle Sam, Louisiana
18. Why, Arizona
19. Whynot, Mississippi
20. Zap, North Dakota

MOST POPULAR NATIONAL PARKS IN THE U.S.

	visitors in 1993	*federal acres**
1. Great Smokey Mountains National Park in North Carolina/ Tennessee	9,283,848	520,000
2. Grand Canyon National Park in Arizona	4,575,602	1,181,000
3. Yosemite National Park in California	3,839,645	760,000
4. Yellowstone National Park in Wyoming	2,912,193	2,220,000
5. Rocky Mountains in Colorado	2,780,342	265,000
6. Olympic National Park in Washington	2,679,598	913,000
7. Acadia National Park in Maine	2,656,034	41,000
8. Grand Teton Park in Wyoming	2,568,689	308,000
9. Mammoth Cave in Kentucky	2,396,234	52,000
10. Zion National Park in Utah	2,391,580	413,000

The U.S. National Parks system includes a total of 45,521,000 federal acres.

IMPORTANT U.S. ADDRESSES

person or organization	address
1. **President of the U.S.**	The White House 1600 Pennsylvania Ave. Washington, D.C. 20500
2. **Vice President**	Admiral House 34th and Massachusetts Washington, D.C. 20005
3. **U.S. Dept. of Education**	400 Maryland Ave. S.W. Washington, D.C. 20202
4. **U.S. Dept. of Energy**	1000 Independence Ave. S.W. Washington, D.C. 20585
5. **U.S. Dept. of Health and Human Services**	200 Independence Ave. S.W. Washington, D.C. 20201
6. **U.S. Dept. of Housing and Human Services**	451 7th St. S.W. Washington, D.C. 20410
7. **Department of Justice**	Constitution Ave. and 10th St. N.W. Washington D.C. 20530
8. **ABA Center on Children and the Law**	1800 M St., N.W. Washington D.C. 20036 (finds lawyers for kids)
9. **Al-Anon/Alkateen**	Family Groups P.O. Box 182 Madison Square Garden Station New York, NY 10159 (help for family and friends of alcoholics)
10. **American Anorexic/ Bulimia Assoc. (AABA)**	418 East 76 St. New York, NY 10021 (help for kids with eating disorders)
11. **Big Brothers/Big Sisters of America**	230 N. 13th St. Philadelphia, PA 19107 (adult support for children without parents)
12. **Boy Scouts of America**	1325 Walnut Hill Ln. Irving, TX 75015
13. **Children of Alcoholic Parents**	23425 N.W. Hwy. Southfield, MI 48075 (a support group)
14. **Girl Scouts of America**	30 East 33rd St. New York, NY 10016
15. **Make-A-Wish Foundation of America**	2600 N. Central Ave., #936 Phoenix, AZ 85004 (wish fulfillment for sick children)

16. **National Center for Missing & Exploited Children**
2102 Wilson Blvd., #550
Arlington, VA 22201
HOTLINE: 1-800-843-5678
(help for runaways and abused children)

17. **National Council on Child Abuse and Family Violence**
1165 Connecticut Ave., N.W.
Washington, D.C. 20036
HOTLINE: 1-800-222-2000
(helps callers find agencies near where they live that offer family counseling)

18. **National Crime Prevention Council**
733 15th St., N.W., Suite 540
Washington, D.C. 20005
(provides information about starting a crime watch program in a community)

19. **National Court Appointed Special Advocates Assoc.**
2722 Eastlake Ave. E.
#220, Seattle, WA 98102
(provides adults who can help and whom you can talk to)

20. **Young Actors Guild**
c/o Aaron White, 120 S. 3rd St.
Connellsville, PA 15425
(works to protect child performers)

WASHINGTON D.C. ATTRACTIONS

1. **The Capitol Building**: Housing the U.S. Congress, this unique building with its large rotunda can be seen from many parts of the city.

2. **Jefferson Memorial**: In honor of Thomas Jefferson, this circular marble building is beautifully lighted from the outside at night.

3. **Lincoln Memorial**: Styled like a Greek temple, this white marble building has a huge statue of Lincoln inside; his Gettysburg Address is carved into one of the walls.

4. **National Archives**: The archives include the original copies of the Declaration of Independence and the Bill of Rights.

5. **National Gallery of Art**: Considered one of the world's greatest art museums, it owns many famous paintings and portraits.

6. **Smithsonian Institute**: The Smithsonian includes 14 museums—such as the National Air and Space Museum and the Museum of Natural History.

7. **Vietnam Veterans' Memorial**: This V-shaped memorial has black granite walls that include the names of more than 50,000 Americans who died in the Vietnam War.

8. **Washington Monument**: In honor of George Washington, this marble pillar, rising to over 555 feet high, offers a great view of the city from the top.

9. **Washington Zoo**: This great zoo offers visitors a rare glimpse of Chinese panda bears.

10. **White House**: Only the public rooms of the President's house can be visited.

FASCINATING FACTS ABOUT THE STATUE OF LIBERTY

1. The statue is 20 times life size.
2. Its statistics are as follows:
   - figure height is 151 feet 1 inch
   - base height is 65 feet
   - pedestal height is 89 feet
   - stands 305 feet above the water
   - weight is 450,000 pounds, or 225 tons
   - mouth is 3 feet wide
   - each eye is $2^1/_2$ feet wide
   - each finger is 8 feet long
   - each fingernail is 10x13 inches long
3. A Frenchman, Frederic Auguste Bartholdi (1834–1904) designed the statue and used his mother as the model for its face.
4. Gustave Eiffel, who built the Eiffel Tower in Paris, built the steel skeleton of the statue from Bartholdi's model, which was only 9 feet tall.
5. The seven spikes on the crown symbolize the seven continents and the seven seas of the world.
6. Inscribed on the tablet that the statue holds is July 4, MDCCLXXVI (1776), the date of American independence.
7. The statue was begun in 1874 and was completed almost a decade later in 1883 at a cost of $600,000. It was then shipped across the Atlantic in pieces and finally reassembled on Bedloes Island in New York Harbor on July 4, 1884.
8. A restoration of the statue, which was begun in 1984, was completed in time for a celebration of the its 100th birthday on July 4, 1986.
9. Originally, the statue was used as a lighthouse.
10. The statue was a gift to the people of the United States from the French people in honor of freedom and democracy.

MOST POPULAR AMUSEMENT PARKS IN THE U.S.*

	location	annual visitors
1. The Magic Kingdom of Walt Disney World	Lake Buena Vista, FL	11,200,000
2. Disneyland	Anaheim, CA	10,300,000
3. EPCOT at Walt Disney World	Lake Buena Vista, FL	9,700,000
4. Disney-MGM Studios at Walt Disney World	Lake Buena Vista, FL	8,000,000
5. Universal Studios, Florida	Orlando, FL	7,700,000
6. Sea World of Florida	Orlando, FL	4,600,000
7. Universal Studios, Hollywood	Universal City, CA	4,600,000
8. Knott's Berry Farm	Buena Park, CA	3,800,000
9. Busch Gardens	Tampa, FL	3,700,000
10. Sea World of California	San Diego, CA	3,700,000

*Based on 1994 estimates

World Geography

CONTINENTS

	sq. mi.	sq. km	population*	% of total world population
1. Africa	11,687,188	30,269,680	654,600,000	12.2
2. Antarctica	5,100,023	13,209,000	none	
3. Asia	17,176,102	44,485,900	3,317,800,000	61.3
4. Australia	3,035,651	7,862,300	17,800,000	0.3
5. Europe	4,065,945	10,530,750	684,400,000	12.6
6. North America	9,357,294	24,235,280	435,800,000	8.1
7. South America	6,880,638	17,820,770	299,900,000	5.5

*based on 1992 statistics

LARGEST DESERTS IN THE WORLD

	approx. sq. mi.	approx. sq. km
1. Sahara in North Africa	3,500,000	9,065,000
2. Great Australian in Australia	1,470,000	3,800,000
3. Great Arabian in southwest Asia	502,000	1,300,000
4. Gobi, covering most of Mongolia	500,000	1,295,000
5. Kalahari in southern Africa	225,000	582,800
6. Takla Makan in China	140,000	362,600
7. Turkestan (Kara Kum) in central Asia	120,000	310,800
8. Thar in northwest India/Pakistan	100,000	259,000
9. Sonoran in U.S./Mexico	70,000	181,300
10. Atacama in northern Chili	70,000	181,300

HIGHEST MOUNTAINS IN THE WORLD*

	ft.	m
1. Everest in Nepal/Tibet	29,028	8,848
2. K2 in Kashmir	28,250	8,611
3. Kanchenjunga in Nepal/Sikkim	28,208	8,598
4. Lhotse in Nepal/Tibet	27,890	8,501
5. Makalu I in Tibet/Nepal	27,790	8,470
6. Dhaulagiri I in Nepal	26,810	8,172
7. Manaslu I in Nepal	26,760	8,156
8. Cho Oyu in Nepal	26,750	8,153
9. Nanga Parbat in Kashmir	26,660	8,126
10. Annapurna I in Nepal	26,504	8,078

*All of the 10 highest mountains—except K2 and Nanga Parbat—are part of the Himalayas.

Origins of State Names • Most Populated Cities • Largest Deserts • Famous World Struct
Largest Countries in the World • Oceans • Important U.S. Addresses • The Statue of Lib

OCEANS

	area		greatest known depth	
	in sq. mi.	in sq. km	in ft.	in m.
1. Arctic	5,440,200	14,090,000	18,456	5,625
2. Atlantic	31,815,000	82,400,000	30,246	9,219
3. Pacific	64,000,000	165,760,000	36,198	11,033
4. Indian	25,300,000	65,526,700	24,460	7,455

FAMOUS MOUNTAINS

	reason for fame
1. Adam's Peak in Sri Lanka	considered sacred by Buddhists, Hindus, and Muslims
2. Mauna Kea in Hawaii	tallest mountain peak at 33,476 feet high, but less than half of it is above ground
3. Mauna Loa in Hawaii	largest active volcanic mountain at 13, 680 feet, including a crater 3 miles long and 1 mile wide
4. Mt. Ararat in Turkey/Iran	according to the Bible, Noah's ark landed here after the flood
5. Mt. Fuji in Japan	most photographed and painted mountain in the world
6. Mt. Huascaran in Peru	first major mountain peak to be climbed by a woman, Annie Peck of Providence, RI, in 1908
7. Mt. Olympus in Greece	known as the "home" of the ancient Greek gods
8. Mt. Rushmore in South Dakota	known for its gigantic sculpture of four U.S. Presidents: Washington, Jefferson, Lincoln, and T. Roosevelt
9. Mt. Sinai in Egypt	according to the Bible, Moses received the Ten Commandments here
10. Mt. Vesuvius in Italy	erupted in 79 A.D. and buried the city of Pompeii

LONGEST RIVERS IN THE WORLD

	mi.	km
1. Nile in Tanzania/Uganda/Sudan/Egypt	4,145	6,673
2. Amazon in Peru/Brazil	4,000	6,440
3. Mississippi-Missouri in U.S.	3,740	6,021
4. Yangtze in China	3,720	5,989
5. Yenisey-Angara in Mongolia/Russia	3,650	5,877
6. Huang He (Yellow River) in China	2,903	4,674
7. Ob-Lrtysh in Mongolia/Kazakhstan/Russia	3,360	5,410
8. Zaïre (Congo) in Angola/Zaïre	2,900	4,669
9. Lena in Russia	2,730	4,395
10. Mekong in Tibet/China/Myanmar (Burma)/ Laos/Cambodia/Vietnam	2,600	4,186

LONGEST RIVERS IN NORTH AMERICA

	mi.	km
1. Mackenzie-Peace in Canada	2,635	4,242
2. Missouri-Red Rock in U.S.	2,533	4,078
3. Mississippi in U.S.	2,348	3,780
4. Yukon in Canada and U.S.	1,979	3,185
5. Rio Grande in U.S.	1,885	3,035
6. Nelson in Canada	1,600	2,576
7. Arkansas in U.S.	1,450	2,335
8. Colorado in U.S.	1,450	2,334
9. Ohio-Allegheny in U.S.	1,300	2,093
10. St. Lawrence in Canada	800	1,288

TALLEST WATERFALLS IN THE WORLD

	ft.	m
1. Angel in Venezuela	3,212	979
2. Tugela in South Africa	3,110	948
3. Utigård in Norway	2,625	800
4. Mongefossen in Norway	2,540	774
5. Yosemite in U.S.	2,425	739
6. Óstre Mardóla Foss in Norway	2,154	657
7. Tyssestrengane in Norway	2,120	646
8. Cuquenan in Venezuela	2,000	610
9. Sutherland in New Zealand	1,904	580
10. Kjellfossen in Norway	1,841	561

LARGEST LAKES IN THE WORLD

	approx. sq. mi.	approx. sq. km
1. Caspian Sea in Azerbaijan/Iran/ Kazakhstan/Russia/Turkmenistan	146,101	378,400
2. Superior in Canada/U.S.	31,699	82,100
3. Victoria in Kenya/Tanzania/Uganda	24,301	62,940
4. Huron in Canada/U.S.	23,004	59,580
5. Michigan in U.S.	22,278	57,700
6. Aral Sea in Kazakhstan/Uzbekistan	15,444	40,000
7. Tanganyika in Burundi/Tanzania/ Zaïre/Zambia	12,350	31,987
8. Baikal in Russia	12,160	31,494
9. Great Bear in Canada	12,023	31,153
10. Great Slave in Canada	11,031	28,570

FAMOUS WORLD STRUCTURES

	location
1. Eiffel Tower	Paris, France
2. Great Sphinx	Giza, Egypt
3. Great Wall	northern China
4. Imperial Palace	Tokyo, Japan
5. Kremlin	Moscow, Russia
6. Leaning Tower of Pisa	Pisa, Italy
7. Parthenon (temple)	Athens, Greece
8. Statue of Liberty	New York City, U.S.
9. Stonehenge	southern England
10. Taj Mahal (tomb)	Agra, India

CANADIAN PROVINCES AND TERRITORIES

	capitals	area sq. mi.	area sq. km
1. Alberta	Edmonton	255,300	661,187
2. British Columbia	Victoria	366,240	948,560
3. Manitoba	Winnipeg	251,014	650,089
4. New Brunswick	Fredericton	28,356	73,437
5. Newfoundland	Saint John's	156,194	404,518
6. Northwest Territories	Yellowknife	1,304,978	3,379,693
7. Nova Scotia	Halifax	21,426	55,491
8. Ontario	Toronto	412,606	1,068,586
9. Prince Edward Island	Charlottetown	2,184	5,567
10. Quebec	Quebec	594,894	1,540,685
11. Saskatchewan	Regina	251,795	651,902
12. Yukon Territory	Whitehorse	207,088	536,326

LARGEST COUNTRIES IN THE WORLD

	capital	area sq. mi.	area sq. km	approx. population
1. Russia	Moscow	6,592,800	17,075,400	147,800,000
2. Canada	Ottawa	3,851,809	9,976,186	29,100,000
3. China	Beijing	3,691,521	9,561,000	1,192,000,000
4. U.S.	Washington, D.C.	3,536,341	9,159,123	260,800,000
5. Brazil	Brasilia	3,286,470	8,511,957	155,300,000
6. Australia	Canberra	2,966,150	7,682,300	17,800,000
7. India	New Delhi	1,229,737	3,185,019	911,600,000
8. Argentina	Buenos Aires	1,072,067	2,776,654	33,900,000
9. Kazakhstan	Alma-Ata (Alamty)	1,049,000	2,717,300	17,100,000
10. Sudan	Khartoum	967,491	2,505,802	28,200,000

ommon Idioms • Parts of Speech • Best Selling Books of All Time • Synonyms • Lite
erms • Abbreviations • Commonly Misspelled Words • Magazines for Young Peop
ommon Suffixes • Steps in the Writing Process • Linking Verbs • Compound Words •
f Speech • Best Selling Books of All Time • Synonyms • Literary Terms • Abbreviation
ommonly Misspelled Words • Magazines for Young People • Common Suffixes • Steps i
Writing Process • Linking Verbs • Compound Words • Parts of Speech

LANGUAGE ARTS

Letters, Words, and Phrases

ABBREVIATIONS

Common Abbreviations

1. assoc. = association
2. co. = company
3. COD = cash on delivery
4. dept. = department
5. etc. = et cetera (and others)
6. FYI = for your information
7. govt. = government
8. inc. = incorporated/incomplete
9. I.O.U. = I owe you
10. lat. = latitude
11. long. = longitude
12. M.O. = money order
13. mph = miles per hour
14. mt. = mountain
15. p. = page (pp. = pages)
16. pl. = plural
17. P.S. = postscript
18. sing. = singular
19. sq. = square
20. v., vs. = versus

Abbreviations with Addresses

1. Ave. = Avenue
2. Blvd. = Boulevard
3. Ct. = Court
4. Hwy. = Highway
5. Pkwy. = Parkway
6. Rd. = Road
7. Rte. = Route
8. Sq. = Square
9. St. = Street
10. Terr. = Terrace

Abbreviations with Calendars

1. Sun. = Sunday
2. Mon. = Monday
3. Tues. = Tuesday
4. Wed. = Wednesday
5. Thurs. = Thursday
6. Fri. = Friday
7. Sat. = Saturday

1. Jan. = January
2. Feb. = February
3. Mar. = March
4. Apr. = April
5. May (none)
6. June (none)
7. July (none)
8. Aug. = August
9. Sept. = September
10. Oct. = October
11. Nov. = November
12. Dec. = December

Abbreviations for States

1. Alabama = AL	26. Montana = MT
2. Alaska = AK	27. Nebraska = NE
3. Arizona = AZ	28. Nevada = NV
4. Arkansas = AR	29. New Hampshire = NH
5. California = CA	30. New Jersey = NJ
6. Colorado = CO	31. New Mexico = NM
7. Connecticut = CT	32. New York = NY
8. Delaware = DE	33. North Carolina = NC
9. Florida = FL	34. North Dakota = ND
10. Georgia = GA	35. Ohio = OH
11. Hawaii = HI	36. Oklahoma = OK
12. Idaho = ID	37. Oregon = OR
13. Illinois = IL	38. Pennsylvania = PA
14. Indiana = IN	39. Rhode Island = RI
15. Iowa = IA	40. South Carolina = SC
16. Kansas = KS	41. South Dakota = SD
17. Kentucky = KY	42. Tennessee = TN
18. Louisiana = LA	43. Texas = TX
19. Maine = ME	44. Utah = UT
20. Maryland = MD	45. Vermont = VT
21. Massachusetts = MA	46. Virginia = VA
22. Michigan = MI	47. Washington = WA
23. Minnesota = MN	48. West Virginia = WV
24. Mississippi = MS	49. Wisconsin = WI
25. Missouri = MO	50. Wyoming = WY

Abbreviations with Time

1. A.D. = *anno domini* "in the year of our Lord"
2. A.M. = *ante meridiem* "before noon"
3. B.C. = before Christ
4. hr. = hour
5. min. = minute
6. mo. = month
7. P.M. = *post meridiem* "after noon"
8. sec. = second
9. wk. = week
10. yr. = year

Abbreviations with Titles

1. Capt. = Captain	6. Maj. = Major
2. Dr. = Doctor	7. Pres. = President
3. Gen. = General	8. Rep. = Representative
4. Gov. = Governor	9. Rev. = Reverend
5. Lt. = Lieutenant	10. Supt. = Superintendent

ACRONYMS*

1. ABC   American Broadcasting Company
2. AIDS   Acquired Immune Deficiency Syndrome
3. ASAP   as soon as possible
4. CBS   Columbia Broadcasting System
5. COD   cash on delivery
6. CPA   certified public accountant
7. DA   district attorney
8. DJ   disc jockey
9. ERA   Equal Rights Amendment
10. IQ   intelligence quotient
11. IRS   Internal Revenue Service
12. NASA   National Aeronautics and Space Administration
13. NBC   National Broadcasting Company
14. PBS   Public Broadcasting Company
15. PS   postscript
16. SADD   Students Against Drunk Driving
17. SOS   Save our ship
18. TLC   tender loving care
19. UFO   unidentified flying object
20. VIP   very important person

Words or names formed by combining the first letters or groups of letters of a series of words.

COMMON PREFIXES

	meaning	example
1. auto-	self, same one	auto + mobile = automobile
2. bi-	two, twice	bi + weekly = biweekly
3. circum-	around	circum + navigate = circumnavigate
4. dis-	not	dis + ease = disease
5. ex-	from, not, former	ex + port = export
6. fore-	in front of, previous	fore + head = forehead
7. il-, im-, in-	not, without	il + legal = illegal
8. inter-	between, together	inter + state = interstate
9. intra-	within, inside	intra + state = intrastate
10. mis-	incorrect	mis + place = misplace
11. multi-	many, more than two	multi + colored = multicolored
12. non-	not	non + stop = nonstop
13. post-	after, later	post + script = postscript
14. pre-	before	pre + historic = prehistoric
15. re-	again	re + pay = repay
16. retro-	backward, back	retro + active = retroactive
17. tele-	far	tele + scope = telescope
18. trans-	across, through	trans + port = transport
19. un-	not	un + cover = uncover
20. uni-	one, single	uni + cycle = unicycle

COMMON SUFFIXES

	meaning	example
1. -able, -ible	fit for, capable	wash + able = washable
2. -ant, -ent	one who performs a certain action	defend + ant = defendant
3. -dom	office, state of being	free + dom = freedom
4. -en	make or become	sharp + en = sharpen
5. -er/-or	one who	teach + er = teacher/act + or = actor
6. -ful	full of, having	care + ful = careful
7. -ment	state of	equip + ment = equipment
8. -some	causing, described as	lone + some = lonesome
9. -ward	in the direction of	home + ward = homeward
10. -y	full of, like, described as	dirt + y = dirty

PARTS OF SPEECH

	abbr.	examples
1. noun	n.	girl, captain, playground, camp, cat, computer
2. pronoun	pron.	he, she, him, her, it, they, them, our, ours, you
3. adjective	adj.	bright, tasty, hot, soft, smooth, dusty, red, lovable
4. adverb	adv.	quickly, now, slyly, yearly, here, tomorrow, orderly
5. preposition	prep.	throughout, except, like, over, past, underneath
6. conjunction	conj.	and, but, or, yet, both/and, either/or, neither/nor
7. interjection	interj.	Ah!, Bah!, Ouch!, Ugh!, Well!, Oh!, Help!, Oops!

KINDS OF PRONOUNS

Personal Pronouns

	singular	plural
1. first person (speaker)	I, me	we, us
	my, mine	our, ours
2. second person (person spoken to)	you	you
	your, yours	your, yours
3. third person (person or thing spoken about)	she, her, hers	they, them
	he, him, his	their, theirs
	it, its	

Indefinite Pronouns

1. all	6. both	11. few	16. one
2. any	7. each	12. many	17. several
3. anybody	8. everybody	13. most	18. some
4. anyone	9. everyone	14. none	19. someone
5. anything	10. everything	15. no one	20. something

Demonstrative Pronouns

1. this   2. that   3. these   4. those

Interrogative Pronouns

1. what   2. which   3. who   4. whom   5. whose

COMMON HELPING VERBS

1. be   am, is, are, was, were, be, being, been
2. have   has, have, had
3. do   do, does, did
4. others   may, might, must, can, could, shall, should, will, would

LINKING VERBS

Common Linking Verbs

1. be	9. can be	17. had been
2. is	10. could be	18. could have been
3. am	11. should be	19. should have been
4. are	12. would be	20. may have been
5. was	13. may be	21. might have been
6. were	14. might be	22. must have been
7. shall be	15. have been	
8. will be	16. has been	

Special Linking Verbs

1. appear	5. look	9. sound
2. become	6. remain	10. stay
3. feel	7. seem	11. taste
4. grow	8. smell	12. turn

COMMON PREPOSITIONS

1. about	11. behind	21. from	31. over
2. above	12. below	22. in	32. through
3. across	13. beneath	23. into	33. to
4. after	14. beside	24. inside	34. toward
5. against	15. between	25. near	35. under
6. along	16. beyond	26. of	36. until
7. among	17. by	27. off	37. up
8. around	18. down	28. on	38. with
9. at	19. during	29. out	39. within
10. before	20. for	30. outside	40. without

SYNONYMS, ANTONYMS, AND HOMONYMS

word	synonym	antonym	homonym
1. above	over	below	
2. aid	help	hinder	aide
3. alike	same	different	
4. alter	change	preserve	altar
5. ate	consumed	fasted	eight
6. back	rear	front	
7. beat	defeat	win	beet
8. begin	start	end	
9. break	shatter	repair	brake
10. bright	brilliant	dim	
11. choose	select	reject	
12. coarse	rough	smooth	course
13. difficult	hard	easy	
14. enlarge	expand	reduce	
15. export	send	import	
16. funny	humorous	serious	
17. great	large	small	grate
18. happy	glad	sad	
19. heal	cure	infect	heel
20. ill	sick	well	
21. like	same	different	
22. little	small	big	
23. made	created	destroyed	maid
24. more	additional	less	
25. none	nothing	all	nun
26. push	shove	pull	
27. real	actual	fake	reel
28. remain	stay	leave	
29. right	correct	wrong	wright, rite, write
30. sent	dispatched	returned	cent
31. strong	powerful	weak	
32. threw	pitched	caught	through
33. to	toward	from	too, two
34. tow	pull	push	toe
35. usual	normal	rare	
36. vacant	empty	full	
37. weak	feeble	strong	week
38. well	healthy	ill	
39. whole	entire	part	hole
40. won	beat	lost	one

COMPOUND WORDS*

1. afternoon
2. backyard
3. baseball
4. birthday
5. breakfast
6. campfire
7. classmate
8. cowboy
9. cupcake
10. downstairs
11. earthquake
12. flashlight
13. fruitcake
14. gentleman
15. goldfish
16. homemade
17. leftover
18. lifeboat
19. motorcycle
20. newspaper
21. outfield
22. pancake
23. peanut
24. popcorn
25. shoelace
26. sunrise
27. Thanksgiving
28. tiptoe
29. weekend
30. wristwatch

Two words put together to form a new word.

ONOMATOPOEIA*

1. bang
2. boom
3. buzz
4. chime
5. clang
6. click
7. crackle
8. croak
9. ding dong
10. fizz
11. growl
12. gurgle
13. hiss
14. hum
15. jingle
16. moo
17. plop
18. pop
19. purr
20. quack
21. sizzle
22. smack
23. snap
24. sniff
25. swish
26. thud
27. thump
28. tick-tock
29. whack
30. zoom

Words that imitate the sounds they represent.

COMMONLY MISSPELLED WORDS

1. absence
2. ache
3. again
4. all right
5. altogether
6. always
7. bargain
8. beautiful
9. believe
10. brief
11. busy
12. calendar
13. corral
14. daily
15. different
16. familiar
17. forty
18. friend
19. genuine
20. guess
21. immigrant
22. instead
23. jealous
24. license
25. lightning
26. misspell
27. neighbor
28. nickel
29. occasion
30. ordinary
31. probably
32. quiet
33. reign
34. responsibility
35. science
36. similar
37. stretch
38. thief
39. truly
40. weird

WINNING WORDS IN THE NATIONAL SPELLING BEE*

word	meaning
1. incisor	a tooth adapted for cutting, located at the apex of the dental arch
2. sarcophagus	limestone used for coffins
3. psoriasis	a chronic skin disease characterized by circumscribed red patches covered with white scales
4. Purim	a Jewish holiday celebrated in commemoration of the deliverance of the Jews from the massacre plotted by Haman
5. luge	a small sled that is ridden in a reclined position and used in competition—such as the Olympics
6. milieu	place, environment
7. odontalgia	a pain in the tooth; toothache
8. staphylococci	a bunch of a certain kind of germ
9. elegiacal	of, relating to, or consisting of two dactylic hexameter lines, the second of which lacks the arses in the third and sixth feet
10. spoliator	one who plunders or steals
11. fibranne	a fabric made of spun-rayon yarn
12. antipyretic	an agent that reduces fever
13. Lyceum	a gymnasium near Athens where Aristotle taught
14. kamikaze	a member of a Japanese air attack corps in World War II, assigned to make a suicidal crash on a target
15. antediluvian	of or relating to the period before the flood described in the Bible

*The National Spelling Bee is held every year for students in 8th grade or lower or under 16 years old. The first prize is $5,000.

FREQUENTLY USED FOREIGN WORDS AND PHRASES

foreign term	language	meaning
1. ad infinitum	Latin	forever
2. avant-garde	French	forward, advanced
3. bon voyage	French	good journey
4. c'est la vie	French	that's life
5. cul de sac	French	dead end
6. et cetera (etc.)	Latin	and others
7. Eureka!	Greek	I've found it!
8. klutz	Yiddish	clumsy person
9. laissez-faire	French	noninterference
10. mañana	Spanish	tomorrow
11. mazel tov	Yiddish	congratulations
12. per diem	Latin	by the day
13. por favor	Spanish	please
14. status quo	Latin	current state of affairs
15. tempus fugit	Latin	time flies

COMMON IDIOMS

idiom	meaning
1. afraid of one's shadow	very easily frightened, jumpy
2. against the grain	to annoy or cause trouble and anger
3. baloney	nonsense, unbelievable, trivial
4. beg off	to ask to be excused from something
5. carry the ball	to take the most important or difficult part of an action or business
6. cut to the quick	to hurt someone's feelings deeply
7. fill one's shoes	to take the place of another person and do as well
8. half-baked	not thought out carefully or thoroughly
9. hold one's tongue	to be silent and not talk
10. John Doe	a name for an unknown person
11. lose sight of	to forget or overlook
12. miss by a mile	to be very wrong about something or to fail badly
13. peter out	to die down gradually or to become tired and unable to go on
14. polish off	to finish completely
15. safe and sound	not harmed, hurt, or damaged in any way
16. skate on thin ice	to take a chance or to risk danger or disapproval
17. take off one's hat to	to give honor, praise, and respect to someone
18. the time is ripe	the best time has come for doing something
19. walk on air	to feel happy and excited about something
20. with bells on	with great enthusiasm; in the best of spirits

ALLITERATIVE TONGUE TWISTERS

1. Barbara Burton burned the brown bread badly.
2. Bob Bolger brought the bear a bit of boiled bacon in a big blue bag.
3. Billy Bailey buttoned his bright brown boots and blue coat before breakfast began.
4. How many cuckoos could a good cook cook if a good cook could cook cuckoos?
5. Double bubble gum bubbles double.
6. The daring duke designed a dreadful plot to dupe the desperate desperado.
7. Even Evan's eaten eighteen eggs!
8. Find Phil for some fine fresh fish.
9. Five frantic fat frogs fled from fifty fierce fishes.
10. Give George his green gloves and gleaming galoshes.
11. Hurry! Here's happy Henry's hungry helper.
12. How high his highness holds his haughty head!
13. Lindy lingered, looking longingly for her lost llama.
14. Now nine nice nannies need new necklaces.
15. Please, Pam, pause patiently for the applause.
16. Shy Sally sat shivering in her slim, shiny silk suit.
17. Please sell me six sea shells from the shimmering sea.
18. The shortstop stopped short of the stunning shot.
19. Ten tiny toads tumbled toward the tremendous tank.
20. Which is the witch that wished the wicked wish?

PROVERBS*

1. One piece of good advice is better than a bag full. (Danish)
2. Anger is the only thing to put off till tomorrow. (Slovakian)
3. To every answer you will find a new question. (Yiddish)
4. The apple does not fall far from the apple tree. (Russian)
5. If you sow arrows, you will reap sorrows. (Philippine)
6. What is bad for one is good for another. (French)
7. Don't play with the bear if you don't want to be bit. (Italian)
8. Beauty is but skin deep. (English)
9. Believe not all you hear; tell not all you believe. (Indian—Tamil)
10. If better were within, better would come out. (Scottish)
11. A caged bird longs for the clouds. (Japanese)
12. To blame is easy, to do better is difficult. (German)
13. A book is a friend. (American)
14. While the boy is small, you can see the man. (Chinese)
15. They brag most that can do least. (English)
16. Don't bite until you know whether it is bread or a stone. (Italian)
17. Buffaloes and bulls fight one another; but flies and mosquitoes die from the fight. (Vietnamese)
18. Do not leave until morning the business of evening. (Turkish)
19. He who buys what he doesn't need steals from himself. (Swedish)
20. A camel does not see its own hump; he sees only the hump of his brother. (Moroccan)
21. Burn a candle at both ends, and it will not last long. (Scottish)
22. A cat is a lion in a jungle of small bushes. (Indian—Hindi)
23. If you lie down with the dogs, you will get up with the fleas. (Yiddish)
24. One door is locked, but another is wide open. (Russian)
25. Everything has its price. (American)

Old, wise sayings that are generally believed to be true.

Reading

BEST SELLING BOOKS OF ALL TIME

1. The *Bible*
2. *Quotations from the Works of Mao T'se-tung*
3. *American Spelling Book* by Noah Webster
4. *The Guinness Book of Records*
5. *The McGuffey Readers* by William Holmes McGuffey
6. *A Message to Garcia* by Elbert Hubbard
7. *The Common Sense Book of Baby and Child Care* by Dr. Benjamin Spock
8. *World Almanac*
9. *Valley of the Dolls* by Jacqueline Susann
10. *In His Steps: "What Would Jesus Do?"* by Rev. Charles Monroe Sheldon

BEST SELLING CHILDREN'S BOOKS IN THE U.S. SINCE 1900

1. *The Tale of Peter Rabbit* by Beatrix Potter
2. *Green Eggs and Ham* by Dr. Seuss
3. *One Fish, Two Fish, Red Fish, Blue Fish* by Dr. Seuss
4. *The Outsiders* by S. E. Hinton
5. *Hop on Pop* by Dr. Seuss
6. *Dr. Seuss's ABC* by Dr. Seuss
7. *The Cat in the Hat* by Dr. Seuss
8. *Are You there, God? It's Me, Margaret* by Judy Blume
9. *The Wonderful Wizard of Oz* by L. Frank Baum
10. *Charlotte's Web* by E. B. White

FAVORITE BOOKS OF MIDDLE SCHOOL STUDENTS*

1. *The BFG* by Roald Dahl
2. *Charlie and the Chocolate Factory* by Roald Dahl
3. *Charlotte's Web* by E. B. White
4. *Honey I Shrunk the Kids* by Hiller and Faucher
5. *Indian in the Cupbard* by Lynne Reid Banks
6. *Island of the Blue Dolphins* by Scott O'Dell
7. *James and the Giant Peach* by Roald Dahl
8. *Superfudge* by Judy Blume
9. *Tales of a Fourth Grade Nothing* by Judy Blume
10. *There's a Boy in the Girls' Bathroom* by Louise Sachar
11. *Where the Red Fern Grows* by Wilson Rawls
12. *Where the Sidewalk Ends* by Shel Silverstein

*Based on a 1990 survey of 300,000 middle school students.

GODS AND GODDESSES IN LITERATURE

	Greek	Roman	god or goddess of
1.	Aphrodite	Venus	love and beauty
2.	Demeter	Ceres/Saturn	agriculture/harvest
3.	Eros	Cupid	love
4.	Helios	Apollo	sun
5.	Hephaestus	Vulcan	fire
6.	Hera	Juno	queen of the gods
7.	Hermes	Mercury	messenger/science/invention
8.	Selene	Luna	moon
9.	Poseidon	Neptune	sea
10.	Zeus	Jupiter/Jove	king of the gods

Common Idioms • Parts of Speech • Best Selling Books of All Time • Synonyms • Literary
Abbreviations • Commonly Misspelled Words • Magazines for Young People • Common S

FAMOUS CHARACTERS IN LITERATURE

1.	Aladdin	the young boy who finds a magic lamp in *Arabian Nights*
2.	Alice	the main character in *Alice and Wonderland* and *Through the Looking Glass* by Lewis Carroll
3.	Becky Thatcher	Tom Sawyer's sweetheart in *Tom Sawyer* by Mark Twain
4.	Black Beauty	the horse in *Black Beauty* by Anna Sewell
5.	Captain Hook	the evil pirate in *Peter Pan*
6.	Casey	the baseball player in "Casey at the Bat" by Ernest Lawrence Thayer
7.	Dorothy	the main character in *The Wonderful Wizard of Oz* by L. Frank Baum
8.	Ebenezer Scrooge	the miser in *A Christmas Carol* by Charles Dickens
9.	Gulliver	the main character in *Gulliver's Travels* by Jonathan Swift
10.	Ichabod Crane	the main character in *The Legend of Sleepy Hollow* by Washington Irving
11.	Jim Hawkins	the boy in *Treasure Island* by Robert Louis Stevenson
12.	Mary Lennox	the female character in *The Secret Garden* by Frances Hodgson Burnett
13.	Meg, Jo, Beth, and Amy,	the four sisters in *Little Women* by Louisa May Alcott
14.	Mowgli	the Indian boy raised by wolves in *Jungle Books* by Rudyard Kipling
15.	Mr. Hyde	the evil character in *The Strange Case of Dr. Jekyll and Mr. Hyde* by Robert Louis Stevenson
16.	Natty Bumpo	the main character in *The Leatherstocking Tales* by James Fenimore Cooper
17	Scheherazade	the queen in *Arabian Nights* who told her husband 1001 stories
18.	Sherlock Holmes	the clever detective in a series of stories by Sir Arthur Conan Doyle
19.	Tinker Bell	the fairy in *Peter Pan* by James Barrie
20.	Watson	Sherlock Holmes's assistant

FAMOUS PLACES IN LITERATURE

1.	Atlantis	a legendary island in the Atlantic Ocean
2.	Camelot	a legendary place where King Arthur and the Knights of the Round Table met. (Now it means an ideal place.)
3.	Lilliput	a place where people only six inches tall lived in *Gulliver's Travels*
4.	Mount Olympus	the mythological home of the gods; an actual Greek mountain
5.	Mudville	the city when Casey struck out
6.	Never-Never Land	a place where no one grows up in the book *Peter Pan*
7.	Oz	the kingdom and home of Oz in *The Wonderful Wizard of Oz*

8. Shangri-La   a place where people are happy and never grow old in *Lost Horizon* by James Hilton
9. Sherwood Forest   the woods where Robin Hood and his band of merry men lived
10. Sleepy Hollow   the village in *The Legend of Sleepy Hollow*

AESOP'S MEMORABLE MORALS

1. A simple life in peace and quiet is better than a luxurious life tortured by fear. "The Town Mouse and the Country Mouse"
2. Little friends may prove to be great friends. "The Lion and the Mouse"
3. Look before you leap. "The Fox and the Goat"
4. A villain may disguise himself, but he will not deceive the wise. "The Cat and the Birds"
5. Necessity is the mother of invention. "The Crow and the Pitcher"
6. It is easy to propose impossible solutions. "The Mice in Council"
7. It is possible to have too much of a good thing. "The Marriage of the Sun"
8. Slow and steady wins the race. "The Hare and the Tortoise"
9. He who plays the fool should not be surprised if he misses the prize. "The Wolf and the Kid"
10. It is easy to despise what you cannot obtain. "The Fox and the Grapes"
11. Do not trust flatterers. "The Fox and the Crow"
12. Don't always believe what you see. "The Wolf in Sheep's Clothing"
13. One good turn deserves another. "The Ant and the Dove"
14. The wisest folks know that it's nice to win, but it's foolish to crow. "The King of the Barnyard"
15. Don't try to be what you are not. "The Jay and the Peacocks"

CAREERS FOR PEOPLE WHO LIKE TO READ

1. annotator
2. archivist
3. author
4. book worker (editor, illustrator, reviewer)
5. magazine worker (editor, illustrator, publisher, writer)
6. bookstore worker
7. Braille transcriber
8. crossword puzzle maker
9. editor (magazine, newspaper, publishing, radio, TV)
10. historian
11. indexer
12. librarian (business, city, government, hospital, school)
13. newspaper reporter
14. proofreader
15. radio/TV worker (disc jockey, newsperson, researcher)
16. reader (cassettes, legislative, letters-to-the-editor)
17. researcher/research assistant
18. storyteller
19. teacher
20. translator

MAGAZINES FOR YOUNG PEOPLE

name and address	description
1. **Biography Today** Omnigraphics, Inc. Penebscot Building Detroit, MI 48225	highlights famous people in such areas as entertainment, government, and sports
2. **Cobblestone** 7 School Street Peterborough, NH 03458	focuses on a specific theme that is related to American history
3. **Dolphin Log** Cousteau Society Membership Center 870 Greenbriar Circle, Suite 402 Chesapeake, VA 23320	explores topics related to oceans, rivers, waterways, and marine life
4. **National Geographic World** 1145 17th and M St. N.W. Washington, D.C. 20036	focuses on articles, poems, artwork, and photographs about the natural world
5. **National Wildlife** National Wildlife Federation 8925 Leesburg Pike Vienna, VA 22184	deals with topics pertaining to wildlife, ecology, and conversation
6. **Plays** 120 Boylston St. Boston, MA 02116	prints original one-act plays that would be interesting for young people
7. **Sports Illustrated for Kids** P.O. Box 830609 Birmingham, AL 35283	includes articles, games, comics, photographs, and interesting information about famous sports stars
8. **3-2-1 Contact** P.O. Box 53051 Boulder, CO 80322	presents science, technology, and nature in an upbeat, appealing way
9. **U*S* Kids** Children's Better Health Institute P.O. Box 7036 Red Oak, IA 51591	includes real-life stories about families, pets, and nature
10. **Zillions** P.O. Box 54861 Boulder, CO 80322	features highly interesting articles about how to get the most for your money

MAGAZINES THAT PUBLISH STUDENTS' WORK*

1. **The Acorn**
   1530 7th St.
   Rock Island, IL 61201

   publishes fiction, nonfiction, and black and white drawings on any subject by young people in grades K-12

2. **Children's Digest**
   P.O. Box 567
   Indianapolis, IN 46202

   publishes stories, poems, and jokes for and by preteens

3. **Creative Kids**
   P.O. Box 6448
   Mobile, AL 36660

   publishes stories, poems, plays, and photographs by young people 5 to 18

4. **Creative with Words**
   P.O. Box 223226
   Carmel, CA 93922

   publishes all kinds of works by young people in grades K-12

5. **Kopper Bear Press**
   P.O. Box 19454
   Boulder, CO 80303

   publishes high-quality fiction, nonfiction, poetry, essays, and novels by young people

6. **The Mcguffy Writer**
   5128 Westgate Dr.
   Oxford, OH 45056

   publishes short stories, essays, poems, songs, and black and white art by young people under the age of 12

7. **Meryln's Pen: The National Magazine of Student Writing**
   P.O. Box 1058
   East Greenwich, RI 02818

   publishes most everything by young people in grades 7-10

8. **Skipping Stones**
   P.O. Box 3939
   Eugene, OR 97403

   publishes most everything by young people ages 7-18—including jokes, recipes, magic tricks, and book and movie reviews

9. **Spark!**
   1507 Dana Ave.
   Cincinnati, OH 45207

   publishes creative works by young people ages 6-12 in its "Show and Tell" column

10. **Stone Soup**
    P.O. Box 83
    Santa Cruz, CA 95063

    publishes stories, poems, personal experiences, book reviews, and art by young people under 13

Within each magazine there are specific directions for sending in material.

DEWEY DECIMAL SYSTEM

1. 000-099 General works (encyclopedias and other reference books)
2. 100-199 Philosophy (how people think and what they believe)
3. 200-299 Religion (including mythology and religions of the world)
4. 300-399 Social sciences (folklore and legends, government, manners and customs, vocations)
5. 400-499 Language (dictionaries, grammars)
6. 500-599 Pure science (mathematics, astronomy, nature study)
7. 600-699 Technology (applied sciences: aviation, building, engineering, homemaking—such as cooking)
8. 700-799 Arts (photography, drawing, painting, music, sports)
9. 800-899 Literature (novels, short stories, plays, poetry)
10. 900-999 History (ancient and modern, geography, travel)

Writing

LITERARY TERMS

word	*meaning*
1. alliteration	when two or more words have the same beginning sound
2. antagonist	the person who opposes or competes with the main character; often the villian
3. autobiography	the story of a person's life that is written by that person
4. ballad	a long narrative poem that tells a story
5. biography	the story of a person's life that is written by a different person
6. character	a person or animal who appears in a work of fiction
7. cliché	an overused idea or statement
8. climax	the high point, or most interesting point, in the plot of a work of fiction
9. comedy	a story that contains humor and ends happily
10. conflict	opposing elements or characters in a plot
11. connotation	ideas and feelings associated with a word beyond its actual meaning
12. denotation	the dictionary meaning of a word
13. denouement	the outcome or solution of a plot
14. dialog	the conversation among characters in stories and plays
15. epic	a long narrative poem that is about a great hero
16. essay	a short written prose work that expresses the author's view on a subject
17. fable	a story with a moral or lesson at the end
18. fiction	any literature about imaginary people and events
19. flashback	jumping backward in the order of a story
20. foreshadow	hints during a story about something that will happen later
21. hero	the character, or protagonist, who solves the problems in a story
22. hyperbole	an exaggeration
23. imagery	words that create strong mental pictures
24. metaphor	the comparison of two things without using the word *like* or *as*
25. onomatopoeia	a word that imitates the sound it represents
26. personification	giving objects or things human characteristics
27. plot	the sequence of events in fiction
28. point of view	perspective from which a story is written
29. rhyme	when two or more words have the same ending sound
30. setting	the time and place of a story
31. simile	the comparison of two things using the word *like* or *as*
32. symbol	a word or object that stands for something else
33. stanza	a group of related lines in a poem, similar to a paragraph in a story
34. theme	the main idea in a piece of literature
35. villain	the "bad guy" in a story

TOPICS TO WRITE ABOUT

1. animals   endangered animals, pets, wild animals, zoos
2. Aztecs   their defeat, food, government, leaders, religion
3. the body   the brain, bones, eyes, diseases, health, needs
4. China   its culture, Great Wall, government, history, people
5. composers   Beethoven, Chopin, Gershwin, Mozart, Stravinsky
6. deserts   animal life, the largest, mining, origins, reclaiming
7. earthquakes   causes, predicting, recent, surviving, worst
8. the environment   acid rain, Earth Day, EPA, ozone layer, pollution
9. food   junk food, milk products, pizza, rice, vegetarians
10. Indians   Hiawatha, Sequoyah, Tecumseh, Trail of Tears
11. inventions   blue jeans, cereal, computers, telephone, zipper
12. presidents   childhoods, Lincoln, their pets, youngest, Washington
13. pyramids   buried treasure, their construction, Giza Pyramids
14. rain forests   destruction, saving, source of medicines, wildlife
15. recycling   glass, need for, plastic, practical suggestions, tires
16. robots   early models, in factories, *2001: A Space Odyssey*
17. Roman Empire   colosseum, gods, Julius Caesar, Romulus and Remus
18. sea life   electric eels, food, largest, most dangerous, starfish
19. space travel   accidents, first animals, space shuttles, space walks
20. women   Susan B. Anthony, Elizabeth Blackwell, Amelia Earhart

BOOK REPORT ALTERNATIVES

1. create a picture essay
2. write a letter to the author
3. create a bulletin board
4. give a demonstration
5. write a newspaper article
6. create a video tape
7. write an editorial
8. write a skit or short play
9. draw a storyboard
10. write a series of diary entries
11. draw a comic strip
12. develop and label a time line
13. create a filmstrip
14. develop a board game
15. tape record an interview
16. give a talk as a character in the book
17. hold a debate
18. create a poster
19. write and illustrate a magazine article
20. write and illustrate a travel brochure
21. make a mobile with labeled parts
22. give an oral report
23. write and illustrate a children's book
24. write a fable
25. draw a map
26. write a poem or a rap song
27. retell a story in your own words
28. write a short biography
29. write a series of entries for a captain's log
30. create and illustrate a chart
31. create a series of cartoons
32. develop a slide show
33. give a TV news report
34. make a model
35. create a time capsule
36. conduct a panel discussion
37. rewrite the ending to a story
38. write a telegram
39. make an outline
40. make a chart that shows similarities and/or differences

STEPS IN THE WRITING PROCESS

1. prewriting: choose and limit a subject, consider purpose and audience, gather and organize information, write an outline
2. drafting: write an introduction, a middle, and a conclusion
3. revising: possibilities include: add, rearrange, delete, substitute, and check for unity, coherence, and emphasis
4. editing: check for errors in spelling, usage, punctuation, and capitalization
5. publishing: possibilities include: display, read aloud, submit, share, and enter in a contest

REVISING AND EDITING CHECKLISTS

Revising
1. **Checking overall structure**
   - Does the paper have a catchy beginning that states the main idea (thesis statement) of the essay?
   - Does it follow a logical order?
   - Do transitions connect the paragraphs?
   - Is there a clear conclusion?
2. **Checking paragraph structure**
   - Does each paragraph include a topic sentence?
   - Are there enough specific details?
   - Does each paragraph end with a clincher sentence?
3. **Checking sentence structure**
   - Are there a variety of kinds of sentences?
   - Do the sentences begin in a variety of ways?
   - Do the sentences vary in length?
   - Are specific words, rather than general words, used?
   - Is the vocabulary appropriate for the audience?
   - Are any figures of speech included?
4. **Checking for emphasis and consistency**
   - Are the main ideas easy to recognize?
   - Are some of the most important ideas at the ends of sentences?
   - Is the paper written throughout from the same point of view?
   - Are the tenses of the verbs consistent?

Editing
5. **Checking for punctuation, capitalization, and spelling**
   - Are there any sentence fragments or run-on sentences?
   - Does each sentence end with an end mark?
   - Does each sentence begin with a capital letter?
   - Do all proper nouns begin with a capital letter?
   - Is an apostrophe used with any noun that shows possession?
   - Is other punctuation used correctly?
   - Are all words spelled correctly?

6. **Checking for form**
  - Is the work typed or printed on $8^1/_2$x11" paper—on one side?
  - Are there 1-inch margins on both sides of each page?
  - Is there a 1-inch margin at the bottom of each page?
  - Is each paragraph indented?
  - Are the pages numbered?
  - Are any footnotes and/or bibliography written correctly?

COMMON PROOFREADING MARKS

		meaning	*example*
1.	∧	insert	We counted ten baloons.
2.		delete	We counted ten ballooons.
3.	#	insert space	We counted tenballoons.
4.	◡	close up	We counted ten bal loons.
5.	∼	transpose	We counted ten balloosn.
6.	≡	capital letter	we counted ten balloons.
7.	/	lower case	We counted ten Balloons.
8.	•••	let it stand	We counted ten balloons.
9.	¶	new paragraph	¶ We counted ten balloons.
10.	no ¶	no new paragraph	no ¶ We counted ten balloons.

PARTS OF A BUSINESS LETTER

1. **heading:** includes the writer's street address; the writer's city, state, and zip code; and the date on which the letter was written (Place a comma between the city and state and between the day and year.)

2. **the inside address:** includes the recipient's name, the company name, the company's street address, and the company's city, state, and zip code (Place a comma between the city and state.)

3. **the salutation:** such as *Dear Mr. Jones:* or *Gentlemen:* (Place a colon after the salutation.)

4. **the body:** presented in a paragraph format

5. **the closing:** such as *Sincerely yours* or *Respectfully yours* (Place a comma after the closing.)

6. **signature:** written in ink and followed by a typewritten name

Roman Numerals • Time • Weight • Area • Math Symbols • Depth • Important Dates
• Time • Weight • Metric System • Math Symbols • Depth • Important Dates • Rom
Numerals • Time • Weight • Metric System • Math Symbols • Weight • Important Date
• Roman Numerals • Time • Weight • Math Symbols • Depth • Important Dates
Roman Numerals • Time • Weight • Chara System • Math Symbols • Depth • Importa
Dates • Roman Numerals • Length • Metric System • Money • Important Area • Mon

MATHEMATICS

Conversions

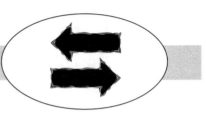

METRIC SYSTEM

Length	value	Capacity	value
1. kilometer (km)	= 1,000 meters	1. kiloliter (kl)	= 1,000 liters
2. hectometer (hm)	= 100 meters	2. hectoliter (hl)	= 100 liters
3. dekameter (dam)	= 10 meters	3. dekaliter (dal)	= 10 liters
4. meter (m)	= 1 meter	4. liter (l)	= 1 liter*
5. decimeter (dm)	= 0.1 meter	5. deciliter (dl)	= 0.10 liter
6. centimeter (cm)	= 0.01 meter	6. centiliter (cl)	= 0.01 liter
7. millimeter (mm)	= 0.001 meter	7. milliliter (ml)	= 0.001 liter

1 liter = 1.057 U.S. quarts

Mass and Weight

1. metric ton	= 1,000,000 grams	6. dekagram	= 10 grams
2. quintal (q)	= 100,000 grams	7. gram	= 1 gram*
3. myriagram	= 10,000 grams	8. decigram	= 0.10 gram
4. kilogram	= 1,000 grams	9. centigram	= 0.01 gram
5. hectogram	= 100 grams	10. milligram	= 0.001 gram

1 gram = 0.035 U.S. ounce

METRIC CONVERSIONS*

When you know:	you can find:	if you multiply by:
Length		
1. inches	millimeters	25
2. feet	centimeters	30
3. yards	meters	0.9
4. miles	kilometers	1.6
5. millimeters	inches	0.04
6. centimeters	inches	0.4
7. meters	yards	1.1
8. kilometers	miles	0.6

When you know:	you can find:	if you multiply by:
Mass		
1. ounces	grams	28
2. pounds	kilograms	0.45
3. grams	ounces	0.035
4. kilograms	pounds	2.2
Liquid Volume		
1. ounces	milliliters	30
2. pints	liters	0.47
3. quarts	liters	0.95
4. gallons	liters	3.8
5. milliliters	ounces	0.034
6. liters	pints	2.1
7. liters	quarts	1.06
8. liters	gallons	0.26

*HELPFUL HINT: *A meter is a little more than a yard. A kilometer is about two-thirds of a mile. A liter is a little more than a quart.*

FRACTION CONVERSIONS

fraction	decimal	percent	fraction	decimal	percent
$1/16$	.00625	6.25%	$9/16$	0.5625	56.25
$1/8$ ($2/16$)	0.125	12.5	$5/8$ ($10/16$)	0.625	62.5
$3/16$	0.1875	18.75	$2/3$	.06	66.6
$1/4$ ($2/8$ or $4/16$)	0.25	25.0	$11/16$	0.6875	68.75
$5/16$	0.3125	31.25	$3/4$ ($6/8$ or $12/16$)	0.75	75.0
$1/3$	.03	33.3	$13/16$	0.8125	81.25
$3/8$ ($6/16$)	0.375	37.5	$7/8$ ($14/16$)	0.875	87.5
$7/16$	0.4375	43.75	$15/16$	0.9375	93.75
$1/2$ ($2/4$, $4/8$ or $8/16$)	.05	50.0	1 ($2/2$, $4/4$, $8/8$ or $16/16$)	1.0	100.0

TEMPERATURE CONVERSIONS

°Fahrenheit		°Centigrade		°Fahrenheit	°Centigrade
212	—boiling point—	100		68	20
194		90		50	10
176		80		32	—freezing point— 0
158		70		14	-10
140		60		-4	-20
122		50		-22	-30
104		40		-40	-40
86		30		-58	-50

Money

INTERNATIONAL FORMS OF MONEY

money	country
1. bolivar	Venezuela
2. cruzeiro	Brazil
3. dinar	Algeria, Jordan, Kuwait, and others
4. dirham	Morocco, United Arab Emirates
5. dollar	Australia, Canada, Hong Kong, New Zealand, Singapore, United States, and others
6. drachma	Greece
7. franc	Belgium, France, Switzerland, and others
8. guilder	Netherlands
9. koruna	Czech Republic, Slovak Republic
10. krona	Iceland, Sweden
11. krone	Denmark, Norway
12. lira	Italy, Turkey
13. mark	Germany
14. peseta	Spain
15. peso	Argentina, Chile, Colombia, Mexico, Philippines, Uruguay, and others
16. pound	Egypt, Great Britain, Lebanon, and others
17. rand	South Africa
18. riyal	Saudi Arabia
19. ruble	Russia
20. rupee	India, Pakistan, and others
21. schilling	Austria
22. won	South Korea
23. yen	Japan
24. yuan	China
25. zloty	Poland

PEOPLE'S FACES ON U.S. MONEY

denomination	portrait
1. 1¢	Abraham Lincoln, 16th President
2. 5¢	Thomas Jefferson, 3rd President
3. 10¢	Franklin Delano Roosevelt, 32nd President
4. 25¢	George Washington, 1st President
5. $1	George Washington, 1st President
6. $5	Abraham Lincoln, 16th President
7. $10	Alexander Hamilton, lst Treasury Secretary
8. $20	Andrew Jackson, 7th President
9. $50	Ulysses S. Grant, 18th President
10. $100*	Benjamin Franklin, U.S. patriot

*Bills larger than $100 were no longer made after 1969. Before then, $500, $1,000, $5,000, and even $100,000 bills had been issued.

Numbers and Symbols

LARGE NUMBERS

	number of zeroes after 1		number of zeroes after 1
1. million	6	6. sextillion	21
2. billion	9	7. septillion	24
3. trillion	12	8. octillion	27
4. quadrillion	15	9. nonillion	30
5. quintillion	18	10. decillion	33

ROMAN NUMERALS

1	I	12	XII	50	L
2	II	13	XIII	60	LX
3	III	14	XIV	70	LXX
4	IV	15	XV	80	LXXX
5	V	16	XVI	90	XC
6	VI	17	XVII	100	C
7	VII	18	XVIII	150	CL
8	VIII	19	XIX	400	CD
9	IX	20	XX	500	D
10	X	30	XXX	900	CM
11	XI	40	XL	1000	M

MATH SYMBOLS

+	addition, plus	∞	infinity	%	percent
∠	angle	∩	intersection (of	⊥	perpendicular
∩	arc		sets)	π	pi
::	as, equal	≐	is approximately	→	ray
@	at		equal to	⌐	right angle
¢	cent	≥	is greater than	{ }	set
Δ	change		or equal to	√	square root
≅	congruent	≤	is less than or	-	subtraction
.	decimal point		equal to	Σ	summation
°	degree	≈	is similar to	∴	therefore 40
÷	divide	:	is to	Δ	triangle
$	dollar	<	less than	≠	unequal
ø	empty set	↔	line	≠	unequilvalent
=	equal	—	line segment	∪	union (of sets)
≈	equivalent 15	×	multiplication	⌐	vector 45
>	greater than	#	number		
ƒ	function	||	parallel 30		

PREFIXES THAT INDICATE NUMBERS

prefix	number	example
1. uni-, mon-, mono-	1	unicycle, monarch, monorail
2. bi-, di-	2	bicycle, binoculars, dissect
3. tri-	3	tricycle, triangle, triplet
4. quadr-, tetr-	4	quadrangle, tetrahedron
5. pent-, penta-	5	pentagon, pentathlon
6. hex-, hexa-	6	hexagon
7. hepta-	7	heptathlon
8. oct-, octa-, octo-	8	octave, octopus, octagon
9. nona-	9	nonagon
10. dec-, deca-	10	decade, decimal
11. cent-	100	century, centipede
12. kilo-	1000	kilogram, kilometer
13. mega-	million	megabyte, megahertz
14. giga-	billion	gigabyte, gigawatt

Time

ORIGINS OF THE NAMES OF DAYS AND MONTHS

Named after

1. Sunday — the sun
2. Monday — the moon
3. Tuesday — Tiu, the Norse god of war
3. Wednesday — Woden, the chief Anglo-Saxon god
4. Thursday — Thor, the Norse god of thunder
5. Friday — Frigga, a Norse goddess
6. Saturday — Saturn, the Roman god of harvests
7. January — Janus, the Roman god of doors and gates
8. February — Februa, the Roman period of purification
9. March — Mars, the Roman god of war
10. April — *aperire*, the Latin word meaning "to open"
11. May — Maia, the Roman goddess of spring and growth
12. June — Juno, the Roman goddess of marriage
13. July — Julius Caesar
14. August — Augustus, the first emperor of Rome
15. September — *septem*, the Latin word for *seven*
16. October — *octo*, the Latin word for *eight*
17. November — *novem*, the Latin word for *nine*
18. December — *decem*, the Latin word for *ten*

DIVISIONS OF TIME

60 seconds	= 1 minute (min.)
60 minutes	= 1 hour (hr.)
24 hours	= 1 day
7 days	= 1 week (wk.)
4 weeks	= 1 month (mo.) (28-31 days)
12 months	= 1 year* (yr.)
4 years	= 1 olympiad
10 years	= 1 decade
20 years	= 1 score
100 years	= 1 century (cen.)
1000 years	= 1 millennium

A year is also 365 days or 52 weeks.

U.S. TIME ZONES*

Zone	Example
1. Eastern Standard Time	noon in New York City, New York
2. Central Standard Time	11:00 a.m. in Chicago, Illinois
3. Mountain Standard Time	10:00 a.m. in Denver, Colorado
4. Pacific Standard Time	9:00 a.m. in San Francisco, California
5. Alaska Standard Time	8:00 a.m. in Juneau, Alaska
6. Hawaii-Aleutian Standard Time	7:00 a.m. in Honolulu, Hawaii

The Earth is divided into 24 times zones, and it takes the sun one hour to cross each zone.

IMPORTANT DATES

		1996	1997	1998	1999
1.	Presidents' Day	Feb. 19	Feb. 17	Feb. 16	Feb. 15
2.	Daylight Savings begins	Apr. 7	Apr. 6	Apr. 5	Apr. 4
3.	National Teacher's Day	May 7	May 6	May 5	May 4
4.	Mother's Day	May 12	May 11	May 10	May 9
5.	Memorial Day	May 27	May 26	May 25	May 31
6.	Father's Day	June 16	June 15	June 21	June 20
7.	Labor Day	Sept. 2	Sept. 1	Sept. 7	Sept. 6
8.	Columbus Day	Oct. 14	Oct. 13	Oct. 12	Oct. 11
9.	Daylight Savings ends	Oct. 27	Oct. 26	Oct. 25	Oct. 31
10.	Thanksgiving Day	Nov. 28	Nov. 27	Nov. 26	Nov. 25

PERIODS OF TIME

1.	annual	= yearly
2.	biannual	= twice a year
3.	bicentennial	= every 200 years
4.	biennial	= every 2 years
5.	bimonthly	= twice a month
6.	biweekly	= twice a week
7.	centennial	= every 100 years
8.	decennial	= every 10 years
9.	diurnal	= daily
10.	fortnight	= two weeks
11.	millennial	= every 1,000 years
12.	quadricentennial	= every 400 years
13.	quincentennial	= every 500 years
14.	semiannual	= every 6 months
15.	semiweekly	= twice a week
16.	thrice weekly	= 3 times a week
17.	trimonthly	= every 3 months
18.	triweekly	= every 3 weeks
19.	undecennial	= every 11 years
20.	vicennial	= every 20 years

Weights and Measures

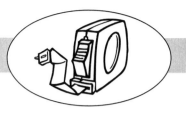

LENGTH

1 foot (ft.)	=	12 inches (in.)
1 yard (yd.)	=	36 inches
1 yard	=	3 feet
1 mile (mi.)	=	5280 feet
1 mile	=	1760 yards
1 league	=	3 miles

AREA

1 square foot (sq. ft.)	=	144 square inches (sq. in.)
1 square yard (sq. yd.)	=	9 square feet
1 square yard	=	1,296 square inches
1 acre	=	4,840 square yards
1 acre	=	43,560 square feet
a square mile (sq. mi.)	=	640 acres

CAPACITY

Dry Measure

1 quart (qt.)	= 2 pints (pt.)
1 peck (pk.)	= 8 quarts
1 bushel (bu.)	= 4 pecks
1 barrel (bbl.)	= 105 quarts

Liquid Measure

1 pint (pt.)	= 16 ounces (oz.)
1 quart (qt.)	= 2 pints
1 quart	= 32 ounces
1 gallon (gal.)	= 4 quarts
1 gallon	= 128 ounces
1 barrel (bbl.)	= $32\frac{1}{2}$ gallons
1 barrel of oil	= 42 gallons

Cooking Measurements

1 teaspoon (tsp.)	= 1/6 fluid ounce (fl. oz.)
1 tablespoon (tbs.)	= 3 teaspoons
1 fluid ounce	= 2 tablespoons
1 cup (c.)	= 16 tablespoons
1 cup	= 8 fluid ounces
1 pint (pt.)	= 2 cups
1 pint	= 16 fluid ounces
1 quart (qt.)	= 4 cups
1 quart	= 2 pints
1 quart	= 32 fluid ounces
1 gallon (gal.)	= 16 cups
1 gallon	= 4 quarts
1 gallon	= 128 fluid ounces

WEIGHT

1 pound (lb.)	= 16 ounces
1 ton (T)	= 2000 pounds

DEPTH

1 fathom	= 6 feet (ft.)
1 cable	= 120 fathoms
1 cable	= 720 feet
1 nautical mile	= 6,076.1 feet

STANDARD MEASUREMENTS

1. most credit cards = $3\frac{3}{8}$ inches wide x $2\frac{1}{8}$ inches long
2. standard business cards = $3\frac{1}{2}$ inches wide x 2 inches long
3. U.S. paper money = $6\frac{1}{8}$ inches wide x $2\frac{5}{8}$ inches long
4. diameter of a quarter = approximately 1 inch
5. standard sheet of paper = $8\frac{1}{2}$ inches wide x 11 inches long

SPECIAL SPEEDS

1. speed of light = 186,000 mph
2. fastest jet = 2,193.167 mph
3. fastest train = 252 mph
4. fastest car = 205 mph
5. peregrine falcon = 175-180 mph
6. sailfish = 68 mph
7. cheetah = 65 mph
8. ostrich = 45 mph
9. fastest human being = 27.89 mph
10. garden snail = 0.03 mph

ANCIENT MATHEMATICAL TERMS

Term	Background
1. acre	An acre, which is 4,840 square yards today, used to be the land that an ox could plow in one day.
2. cubit	A cubit, which is 18 inches today, used to be the distance from the elbow to the fingertips in ancient Egypt.
3. foot	A foot, which is 12 inches today, was originally based on the length of a person's actual foot.
4. hand	A hand, which is used today to measure horses, is 4 inches. Originally, however, it was about 5 inches, or 5 fingers across.
5. inch	An inch was once the width of a man's thumb. Then in the 14th century, King Edward I of England ruled that 1 inch should equal 3 grains of barley placed end to end lengthwise.
6. lick	The Greeks used a lick to measure the distance from the tip of the thumb to the tip of the index finger.
7. marathon	In Ancient Greece the first marathon runner was a soldier who ran 26 miles from the battle at Marathon to Athens to report that the war had been won. (As soon as he delivered his message, he collapsed and died.) Today the race is 26 miles and 385 yards.
8. pace	A pace, which is the length of one step of $2\frac{1}{2}$ to 3 feet, used to be the length of the ancient Roman soldiers' double step as they marched, which was about 5 feet. At 5 feet, 1,000 paces equaled a mile.
9. span	Originally, a span was the length of the hand stretched out, which was then about 9 inches.
10. yard	A yard, which is 36 inches today, used to be the length of a man's belt. In the 12th century, King Henry I of England officially established the yard as the distance from his nose to the thumb of his outstretched arm.

SPECIAL WEIGHTS*

1. blue whale	= 143 tons
2. African elephant	= $7\frac{1}{2}$ tons
3. hippopotamus	= $4\frac{1}{2}$ tons
4. Indian rhinoceros	= $3\frac{1}{4}$ tons
5. cow	= 1,500 pounds
6. pig	= 400 pounds
7. cat	= 9 pounds
8. African ostrich egg	= $3\frac{1}{4}$ pounds
9. pygmy shrew	= .07 ounces
10. hummingbird egg	= .02 ounces

*averages

Earth Science • Animals • Kinds of Doctors • Weather and Climate • Inventors • Junk Food
• Extinct Species • Allergies • Rain Forest • Earth Science • Animals • Kinds of Doctor
• Weather and Climate • Inventors • Junk Food • Extinct Species • Allergies • Rain Fore
• Earth Science • Animals • Kinds of Doctors • Weather and Climate • Inventors • Jun
Food • Extinct Species • Allergies • Rain Forest • Earth Science • Animals • Kinds
Doctors • Weather and Climate • Inventors • Junk Food • Extinct Species • Allergies • Rai

SCIENCE

Branches of Science

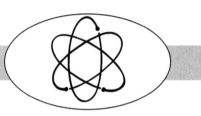

EARTH SCIENCES

	The study of
1. geology	rocks, earthquakes, volcanoes, and fossils
2. meteorology	the atmosphere and weather
3. oceanography	waves, tides, currents, trenches, and ocean life
4. paleontology	plant and animal fossils

LIFE SCIENCES

	The study of
1. anatomy	human structure, form, and the arrangement of the body
2. bacteriology	bacteria: their growth and behavior
3. biology	animals and plants: their origin, morphology, and environment
4. botany	the plant world
5. ecology	the relationship between living things and their environment
6. medicine	the cause, prevention, and cure of disease
7. nutrition	the supply of adequate and correct foods to satisfy the body's requirements
8. pharmacology	drugs: their preparation, use, and effects
9. physiology	the function of living things
10. psychology	the behavior of humans and animals and the working of their brains
11. zoology	animal life

MATHEMATICAL SCIENCES

	The study of
1. computing	the use of computers in mathematics and statistics
2. logic	reasoning—especially as applied to and using mathematics
3. mathematics	the application of geometry, algebra, and arithmetic to concrete data
4. statistics	numerical information and its analysis

PHYSICAL SCIENCES

	The study of
1. astronomy	heavenly bodies and their motions
2. chemistry	the properties and behavior of substances
3. electronics	the behavior of electrons in a vacuum, in gases, and in semiconductors
4. engineering	the application of scientific principles to industry
5. mechanics	the invention and construction of machines: their operation and the calculation of their efficiency
6. metallurgy	the working of metals: smelting and refining
7. physics	the nature and behavior of matter and energy

SOCIAL SCIENCES

	The study of
1. anthropology	the origin, culture, development, and distribution of humans
2. archaeology	the remains and monuments left by earlier people
3. economics	the production, distribution and use of goods and services
4. geography	the location of the Earth's features and the relationship of people to them
5. linguistics	languages and their relationship to each other
6. political science	the function of states and governments
7. sociology	the relationship between groups and individuals

Animals

HEAVIEST LAND ANIMALS

	Average Weight*		Average Length	
	lb.	kg	ft.	m
1. African elephant	11,023	5,000	23.6	7.2
2. Great Indian rhinoceros	8,818	4,000	13.8	4.2
3. hippopotamus	4,409	2,000	16.1	4.9
4. giraffe	2,646	1,200	19.0	5.8
5. American bison (buffalo)	2,205	1,000	12.8	3.9
6. grizzly bear	1,720	780	9.8	3.0
7. Arabian camel (dromedary)	1,323	600	9.8	3.0
8. moose	1,312	595	9.8	3.0
9. tiger	661	300	9.2	2.8
10. gorilla	485	220	6.6	2.0

*The weight of one African elephant was recorded as 13,228 lb. (6,000 kg).

FASTEST ANIMALS

Maximum Recorded Speed

	mph	km/h
1. cheetah	65	105
2. Pronghorn antelope	55	89
3. Mongolian gazelle	50	80
4. Springbok gazelle	50	80
5. Grant's gazelle	47	76
6. Thomson's gazelle	47	76
7. brown hare (rabbit)	45	72
8. horse	43	69
9. greyhound (dog)	42	68
10. red deer	42	68

LONGEST-LIVED ANIMALS

Maximum Age (years)

1. quahog (marine clam)	up to 200	6. lake sturgeon	82
2. giant tortoise	150	7. sea anemone	80
3. Greek tortoise	110	8. elephant	78
4. killer whale	90	9. freshwater mussel	75
5. European eel	88	10. Andean condor	70

MOST INTELLIGENT MAMMALS*

1. chimpanzee	6. monkey
2. gorilla	7. smaller toothed whale
3. orangutan	8. dolphin
4. baboon	9. elephant
5. gibbon	10. pig

Humans, of course, are at the top of this list.

FAMOUS MIGRATIONS

Flyers	Distance	To and from
1. Arctic tern*	25,000 miles, round trip	Arctic to South America or Africa
2. bat	2,400 miles, round trip	Labrador to Bermuda
3. golden plover	16,000 miles, round trip	Canada to South America
4. Monarch butterfly	2,000 miles, round trip	Canada to California
5. wandering albatross	20,000 miles	circles the world, west to east

Swimmers	Distance	To and from
1. Alaskan fur seal	9,000 miles, round trip	Pribilof Islands to the coast of California (the Bering Sea)
2. Atlantic salmon	6,000 miles in the ocean, round trip	St. Lawrence River to Atlantic Ocean
3. dogfish	2,500 miles, round trip	coast of Canada to the Mediterranean
4. emperor penguin	1,000-2,000 miles	Antarctica to Weddell Sea
5. green turtle	2,800 miles, round trip	South America to Ascension Island in the Atlantic Ocean
6. humpback whale	8,000 miles, round trip	Indian Ocean to Atlantic Ocean

Walkers	Distance	To and from
1. bison	800 miles	roam around the northern provinces of Canada
2. caribou	800 miles	Northwest Territories to islands in the Arctic Circle
3. elk	200 miles	roam around the northern provinces of Canada

*The Arctic tern gets the award for the greatest migration of any category.

ANIMAL NAMES

	Group Names	Young
1. bear	sleuth	cub
2. cat	cluster	kitten
3. chicken	clutch, brood	chick
4. cow	herd	calf
5. deer	herd	fawn
6. dog	pack, kennel	puppy, whelp
7. elephant	herd	calf
8. fox	skulk	cub
9. goat	herd	kid
10. goose	flock, gaggle	gosling
11. horse	herd	foal
12. kangaroo	mob	joey
13. lion	pride	cub
14. pig	drove, litter	piglet
15. rabbit	warren	bunny, kit
16. seal	pod	pup
17. sheep	flock	lamb
18. turkey	rafter	poult
19. whale	school, pod	calf
20. wolf	pack	cub, whelp

Ecology

AN ENVIRONMENTAL VOCABULARY

Word	Meaning
1. acid rain	rain that contains acid caused from pollution; it is responsible for killing forests and bodies of water and damaging crops
2. air pollution	harmful substances deposited into the air that cause unhealthy living conditions
3. biodegradable	a substance or material that can be broken down into simpler compounds by natural processes
4. chlorofluoro-carbons (CFCs)	a group of chemicals that contain chlorine, fluorine, and carbon, often used in air conditioning and cleaning products; CFCs are responsible for destroying the ozone layer of the atmosphere that protects the earth
5. climate	the average weather of a particular place
6. compost heap	a pile of food scraps and yard waste that eventually decays and can then be used to enrich the soil
7. conservation	the use of natural resources in a way that assures they will be available for future generations
8. deforestation	the clearing of forest land to be used for something besides a forest
9. ecosystem	a community of living things and the place where they live—such as a forest or lake
10. environment	the totality of one's surroundings—air, water, land, people, and animals—that influences life and how it is lived
11. EPA	U.S. Environmental Protection Agency, which is charged with the protection of the environment through federal regulations
12. extinction	the disappearance of a type (species) of plant or animal from the earth
13. global warming	an increase in the earth's temperature due to the buildup of certain gases in the atmosphere; this condition is caused by pollution
14. greenhouse effect	a condition in which the earth's atmosphere traps heat in the same way as greenhouse glass; too much heat causes global warming
15. habitat	the natural home of an animal or plant
16. hazardous waste	anything thrown away that is harmful to human beings and the environment
17. landfill	a dump, or low area of land that is filled with garbage; there is concern about the time when all the landfills will be filled
18. nonrenewable	a natural resource that cannot be naturally restored or replenished
19. pollution	contamination of air, water, or soil by materials that can injure health, the quality of life, or the working of ecosystems
20. recycle	to separate certain materials from waste so that they can be used again in a similar form or made into something else; recycling saves natural resources (energy, trees, water) and reduces air and water pollution

FASCINATING FACTS ABOUT ECOLOGY

1. Household trash generally consists of 39% paper, 15% yard waste, 10% food waste, 9% plastic, and 27% of a combination of wood, glass, metals, etc.
2. The worldwide release of carbon dioxide from just the burning of fossil fuels totals about 22 billion tons a year.
3. Burning one gallon of gasoline produces two pounds of carbon dioxide.
3. An airplane generates a half a pound of carbon dioxide per passenger per mile.
4. The average per capita production of carbon dioxide in North America is five tons a year.
5. According to the 1990 census, there are almost 6 billion people on the earth, but that figure is expected to double within the next 60 years.
6. Americans use about 600 pounds of paper per person per year, but less than 30% is recycled. However, Japanese recycle 95% of their newspapers, 55% of their steel, 66% of their bottles, and 40% of their aluminum.
7. In just one year, America buries enough metals to build two million cars and enough wood to construct one million houses.
8. In the United States, more than 7.6 million television sets, each loaded with recyclable parts and materials, are thrown out every year.
9. Enough aluminum to build 500,000 mobile homes is thrown away in the United States every year.
10. Publishing the Sunday edition of *The New York Times* newspaper consumes 10,000 trees each week.
11. Recycling one ton of old newspapers saves 17 trees.
12. The United States creates more than 432,000 tons of garbage each day.
13. It costs $20 billion each year for the United States to process its garbage.
14. Styrofoam takes thousands of years to decompose, yet the United States makes 25 billion styrofoam containers each year—most of which ends up in landfills.
15. Nineteen trillion gallons of waste are dumped directly into the oceans each year. That's almost 2,000 times the amount dumped into the ocean in the *Exxon Valdez* oil accident.

SOME ENDANGERED SPECIES

Mammals	Location
1. bobcat	Central Mexico
2. brown bear	U.S. (48 contiguous states)
3. cheetah	Africa to India
4. eastern cougar	Eastern North America
5. Chinese River dolphin	China
6. Asian elephant	Southcentral and Southeast Asia
7. gorilla	Central and West Africa
8. leopard	Africa, Asia
9. giant panda	China
10. gray whale	North Pacific Ocean

Birds	**Location**
11. California condor	U.S. (Oregon and California)
12. hooded crane	Japan
13. bald eagle	U.S. and Canada
14. golden parakeet	Brazil
15. Australian parrot	Australia

Reptiles and Fishes	**Location**
16. American alligator	Southeast U.S.
17. American crocodile	U.S. (Florida)
18. Atlantic Salt Marsh snake	U.S. (Florida)
19. Yaqui catfish	U.S. (Arizona)
20. Gila trout	U.S. (Arizona and New Mexico)

EXTINCT SPECIES*

At least 50 species of birds, including
1. Dodo (1681)
2. Great Auk (1844)
3. Passenger pigeon (1914)
4. Carolina parakeet (1914)
5. Labrador duck (?)

At least 75 species of mammals, including
6. Steller's sea cow
7. Guagga (a type of Zebra)
8. Przewalski's horse
9. European bison
10. Sea mink

Caused by human activities over the last 350 years

RAIN FOREST FACTS

1. Rain forests are often called the "lungs" of the planet because the trees "breathe" so much oxygen into the atmosphere.
2. When the trees in the rain forests are burned, huge amounts of carbon dioxide are released into the air. Too much carbon dioxide could cause the earth to heat up.
3. Every second another acre of tropical rain forest is destroyed.
4. An area the size of Nebraska (76,000 square miles) of rain forest is destroyed every year in just Brazil alone.
5. Rain forests account for only 6% of the earth's land surface, but they contain 50% of the earth's trees.

6. The United States imports about $2.2 billion worth of rain forest hardwood per year; these purchases encourage the destruction of the trees.

7. Scientists have predicted that nearly all of the earth's tropical rain forests will either be destroyed or seriously damaged by the year 2035 if the rate of destruction to the trees continues as it is today.

8. Most rain forests are found in the tropics bordering either side of the equator—like a wide belt circling the earth.

9. Rainfall in the rain forests averages from 100 to 400 inches each year. (In comparison, the rainfall in a city such as Wichita, Kansas, averages about 29 inches a year.)

10. As they compete for sunlight, trees in the rain forests often grow to amazing heights—50 to 150 feet—before sprouting branches and leaves.

11. Currently nearly 2 million species have been discovered and named in the rain forests, and scientists believe that for every known species, there remain 40 yet undiscovered.

12. Dr. Fred Kuntz, a mammal expert at the Bronx Zoo in New York, has said, "We know more about distant planets than we do about the nearest rain forest."

13. Although rain forests account for only 6% of the earth, they are home to more than half of all living things on this planet. As a result of the destruction of the rain forests, many of these species are dying out.

14. Nearly 10,000 species are being lost every year, and they can never be replaced.

15. It takes only a few minutes for a chain saw to cut down a 7-foot-wide tree in the rain forest, but it would take 5 centuries for another tree to grow to the same size.

16. One quarter of all prescription drugs used in the U.S. are made from tropical forest plants.

17. Many fruits, nuts, spices, coffee, sugar cane, and cocoa also originated in rain forests.

18. Rain forests provide Americans with burlap, rope, nets, fibers for stuffing life jackets, and many oils for perfumes.

19. Even the wax that prevents M&M's from melting on your fingers comes from tropical forests.

20. If you are interested in knowing what you can do to help save the rain forests, write to World Wildlife Fund/Conservation Foundation, 1250 24th Street, N.W., Washington, D.C. 20006 or Rainforest Alliance, 295 Madison Avenue, New York, NY 10017.

Food and Nutrition

ESSENTIAL VITAMINS

Vitamin	Found in	Needed for
1. A	milk, butter, eggs, green vegetables, fish oil, liver, and carotene in carrots	fighting disease and seeing in the dark
2. B_1	yeast and wheatgerm (whole wheatbread)	All B vitamins are needed for a healthy appetite, energy, and
3. B_2	yeast	healthy nerves and skin.
4. 9 other B vitamins	milk, meat, and green vegetables	
5. C	oranges, lemons, tomatoes, black currants, strawberries, and fresh vegetables	healthy blood and gums, healing wounds, and possibly protection from colds
6. D	cod-liver oil, cream, egg yolks (and with sunlight, fat below the skin forms vitamin D)	strong bones and teeth
7. E	wheatgerm oil, legumes (such as peas and beans), and nuts	normal reproduction and muscle development
8. K	green vegetables and liver	blood clotting

MOST POPULAR JUNK FOOD*

Starting with the most popular.

1. pizza
2. chicken nuggets
3. hot dogs
4. cheeseburgers
5. macaroni and cheese
6. hamburgers
7. spaghetti and meatballs
8. fried chicken
9. tacos
10. grilled cheese sandwiches

*Nearly $8 billion is spent every year on junk food—
even though none of it is very healthy.*

BRAIN FOOD*

1. apples
2. broccoli
3. fish
4. grapes
5. lean beef
6. lowfat yogurt
7. nuts
8. peaches
9. peanuts
10. pears
11. skim milk
12. turkey breast

*These foods won't actually make people smarter, but they will keep them alert. Foods like
candy, bread, and sugar, on the other hand, make people sleepy and inattentive.*

THE FOOD PYRAMID

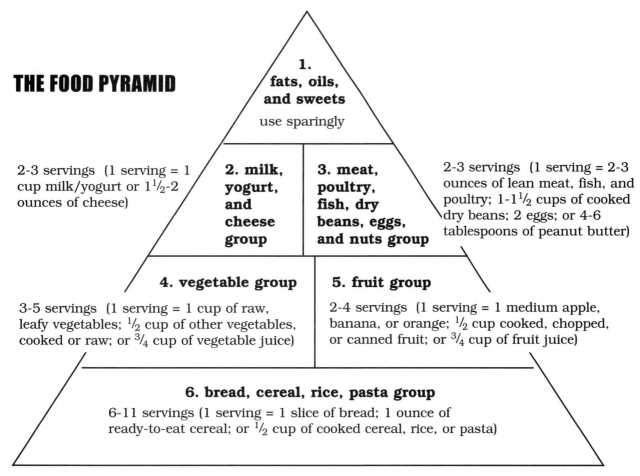

1. fats, oils, and sweets
use sparingly

2-3 servings (1 serving = 1 cup milk/yogurt or 1½-2 ounces of cheese)

2. milk, yogurt, and cheese group

3. meat, poultry, fish, dry beans, eggs, and nuts group

2-3 servings (1 serving = 2-3 ounces of lean meat, fish, and poultry; 1-1½ cups of cooked dry beans; 2 eggs; or 4-6 tablespoons of peanut butter)

4. vegetable group

5. fruit group

3-5 servings (1 serving = 1 cup of raw, leafy vegetables; ½ cup of other vegetables, cooked or raw; or ¾ cup of vegetable juice)

2-4 servings (1 serving = 1 medium apple, banana, or orange; ½ cup cooked, chopped, or canned fruit; or ¾ cup of fruit juice)

6. bread, cereal, rice, pasta group
6-11 servings (1 serving = 1 slice of bread; 1 ounce of ready-to-eat cereal; or ½ cup of cooked cereal, rice, or pasta)

Developed by the U.S. government to help people choose the right foods for good health.

CALORIES IN COMMON FOODS

	Calories
1. apple (1 small)	58
2. bacon (4 slices)	692
3. banana (1 medium)	110
4. bread (1 slice of white)	73
5. Burger King's double whopper with cheese	951
6. butter (1 tablespoon)	100
7. egg (1 large fried)	95
8. grapefruit (½)	42
9. Hershey's chocolate bar	706
10. hotdog (1 cooked)	145
11. Jell-O (½ cup)	97
12. KFC's original recipe (1 drumstick)	117
13. mayonnaise (1 tablespoon)	100
14. McDonald's egg McMuffin	353
15. McDonald's french fries (large)	362
16. McDonald's quarter pounder with cheese	518

	Calories
17. milk (1 cup whole)	150
18. orange (1)	60
19. peanut butter and jelly sandwich	374
20. Pizza Hut's thick n' chewy cheese pizza (2 slices of a medium pizza)	450
21. popcorn (1 cup air-popped)	30
22. potato (1 baked)	220
23. potato chips (10 medium)	105
24. rice (½ cup cooked white)	113
25. salad dressing (1 tablespoon of Italian)	75
26. soup (1 cup of canned chicken noodle)	75
27. sugar (1 teaspoon)	25
28. Taco Bell taco	159
29. vanilla ice cream (1 cup)	290
30. Wendy's double hamburger with cheese	797

INTERESTING FOOD FACTS

1. The average teenager eats about 1,817 pounds of food in a year.

2. Americans, who eat an average of 42 quarts of popcorn a year, consume more popcorn than any other people in the world.

3. It could be said that the ancient Chinese invented ice cream because they were the first to add flavoring to snow and eat it.

4. The first pizza parlor in America opened in New York City in 1905.

5. Jell-O flavors that flopped over the years are apple, cola, celery, mixed vegetables, and salad.

6. Dark brown is the most common color in a bag of M&M's.

7. Doughnuts have been known as bellysinkers, doorknobs, dunkers, flatcakes, burl cakes, cymbals, fried cakes, and sinkers.

8. Hershey Bars were first sold in 1894, but Reese's Pieces were first sold only in 1978.

9. Raisins are actually grapes that have been dried by the sun or artificial heat.

10. A regular 12-ounce soft drink can contain as much as 9 teaspoons of sugar.

11. All of the following foods were created in America: chop suey, English muffins, French fries, Russian dressing, and Swiss steak.

12. All of the following foods were brought to America by immigrants from Europe and Africa: apples, cabbage, carrots, lettuce, oranges, peaches, pears, watermelons, and wheat.

13. An average American who lives to be 70 years old will eat on an average of 880 chickens, 14 beef cattle, 23 hogs, 35 turkeys, 12 sheep, and 770 pounds of fish.

14. Apples are 84% water.

15. A pharmacist in Atlanta, Georgia, invented the syrup for coca-cola in 1886 as a cure for headaches and hangovers. However, a worker in his store created the first Coke when he added carbonated water to the syrup.

16. The first major hamburger chain restaurant, which started in 1921, was White Castle. It offered a thin $2\frac{1}{2}$-inch square hamburger for 5¢.

17. Honey is the only food that does not spoil; honey found in Egyptian tombs tasted very good—even after sitting for thousands of years.

18. A honeybee has to leave the hive 154 times to make just one teaspoon of honey.

19. In the 1830s, a company in the U.S. sold ketchup as a medicine called Dr. Mile's Compound Extract of Tomato.

20. Rice is the main food for half the people of the world.

Inventions

A TIME LINE OF MAJOR INVENTIONS

Year Patented*	Invention	Inventor
1794	cotton gin	Eli Whitney
1803	steamboat	Robert Fulton
1827	matches (friction)	John Walker
1827	washing machine	Chester Stone
1834	refrigeration	Jacob Perkins
1836	revolver	Samuel Colt
1839	rubber, vulcanized	Charles Goodyear
1840	telegraph signs	Samuel F. Morse
1846	sewing machine	Elias Howe
1849	safety pin	Walter Hunt
1852	elevator with a braking device	Elisha Otis
1868	tape measure	Alvin J. Fellows
1869	vacuum cleaner	Ives McGaffey
1871	suspenders	Samuel Clemens (Mark Twain)
1874	barbed wire	Joseph Glidden
1876	telephone	Alexander Graham Bell
1877	phonograph	Thomas A. Edison
1877	microphone	Emile Berliner
1879	cash register	James Ritty
1884	photo film (transparent)	George Eastman
1888	ball point pen	John J. Loud
1889	aspirin	Hermann Dresser
1892	motion picture projector	Thomas A. Edison
1892	ironing board	Sarah Boone
1893	zipper	Whitcomb Judson
1894	submarine (even keel)	Simon Lake
1895	diesel engine	Rudolf Diesel
1901	"motor carriage"	Henry Ford
1903	airplane with a motor	Orville and Wilbur Wright
1911	air conditioner	Willis Carrier
1913	X-ray tube	William Collidge
1925	modern cosmetics	George Washington Carver
1926	rocket engine	Robert H. Goddard
1928	electric razor	Jacob Schick
1930	packaged frozen foods	Clarence Birdseye
1930	television	Philo T. Farnsworth
1933	FM radio	Edwin Armstrong
1938	xerography (instant copying)	Chester Carlson
1947	transistor	John Burdeen
		William Shockley
		Walter Brattain

Year Patented*	Invention	Inventor
1948	Polaroid film	Edwin Land
1955	nuclear reactor	Enrico Fermi
		Leo Szilard
1958	laser	Arthur Schawlow
		Charles H. Townes
1960	videotape recorder	Charles P. Ginsburg
		Shelby Anderson, Jr.
		Ray Dolby

A patent gives the inventor "the right to exclude others from making, using, or selling the invention throughout the United States" for 17 years.

INVENTORS' HALL OF FAME*

Name	Nationality	Dates	Invention
1. Alexander Graham Bell	Scottish/ American	1874-1922	telephone
2. Clarence Birdseye	American	1886-1956	preserving food by freezing
3. Louis Braille	French	1809-1852	system of raised-point writing for use by the blind
4. William Seward Burroughs	American	1855-1898	calculating machine
5. Willis Haviland Carrier	American	1876-1950	air-conditioning system
6. George Washington Carver	American	1864-1943	300 uses for peanuts and 118 sweet potato by-products
7. John Deere	American	1804-1886	haying machine
8. Rudolf Diesel	German	1858-1913	internal combustion engine
9. George Eastman	American	1854-1932	method and tools needed for coating plates for use in photography, motion picture film, and the Kodak camera
10. Thomas Alva Edison	American	1847-1931	electric lamp, phonograph, mimeograph, motion picture cameras and projectors, among a total of 1,093 inventions
11. Alexander Fleming	British	1881-1955	penicillin
12. Benjamin Franklin	American	1706-1790	bifocal lens, heating stove, and lightning rod
13. Henry Ford	American	1863-1947	numerous mechanisms used in cars

Name	Nationality	Dates	Invention
14. Jay W. Forrester	American	1918-	magnetic storage of information, making him a pioneer in the development of electronic computers
15. Charles P. Ginsburg	American	1920-	VCR
16. Charles Goodyear	American	1800-1860	improvements in India-rubber products
17. Samuel B. Morse	American	1791-1872	telegraph signals
18. Elisha Graves Otis	American	1811-1861	passenger elevator
19. Louis W. Parker	Hungarian/ American	1906-	television receiver
20. Louis Pasteur	French	1822-1895	pasteurization
21. Igor I. Sikorsky	Russian/ American	1889-1930	helicopters
22. James Starley	English	1830-1881	modern bicycle
23. George Westinghouse	American	1846-1914	safety devices for railroads
24. Eli Whitney	American	1765-1825	cotton gin
25. Orville and Wilbur Wright	American	1871-1948 1867-1912	flying machine

Robert Patch is the youngest inventor to get a patent. In 1962, at the age of 5, he received a patent for a toy truck.

UNUSUAL INVENTIONS

1. eye protectors for chickens so that they don't peck each other
2. a thief-proof bicycle that shoots needles out of the seat when the owner isn't riding it
3. an alarm clock that drops wooden blocks on the heads of hard-to-wake sleepers
4. bird diapers so that birds can fly around a room without making a mess
5. a hat with a parachute attached so that a person could jump out of a burning building and float safely to the ground
6. a false tooth that is filled with a breath freshener
7. a locker that can store partially chewed gum
8. shoes with the toes in the back and the heels in the front so that soldiers going in one direction will leave tracks that appear to be going in the opposite direction
9. a twirling spaghetti fork to make winding spaghetti easy
10. a sleeping bag that has openings for arms and legs to allow a camper inside the bag to run away in case a bear comes along

Medicine and Health

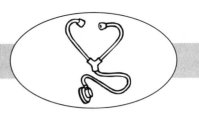

KINDS OF DOCTORS

	Expertise
1. allergist	treats allergies
2. anesthesiologist	puts patients to sleep before surgery
3. cardiologist	treats heart ailments
4. dermatologist	treats skin diseases
5. endocrinologist	treats the glands, such as the thyroid
6. gastroenterologist	specializes in diseases and disorders of the digestive system
7. gynecologist	treats the reproductive system in females
8. hematologist	treats blood diseases
9. immunologist	specializes in the body's defense system against infection and disease
10. nephrologist	treats kidney disorders
11. neurologist	treats the nervous system
12. obstetrician	cares for women during pregnancy
13. ophthalmologist	treats eye diseases
14. orthopedist	treats bone and muscle disorders
15. otolaryngologist	treats ear, nose and throat ailments
16. pathologist	studies the cause, development, and manifestations of disease
17. pediatrician	specializes in the care and treatment of infants and young children
18. radiologist	interprets X-rays of body parts and organs
19. rheumatologist	treats diseases of body joints
20. urologist	treats the urinary tract of the body

MOST COMMON ALLERGIES

From Food	*From the Environment*
1. nuts	1. dust mites in the house
2. shellfish and seafood	2. grass pollens
3. milk	3. tree pollens
4. wheat	4. cats
5. eggs	5. dogs
6. fresh fruit	6. horses
7. fresh vegetables	7. molds
8. cheese	8. birch pollen
9. yeast	9. weed pollen
10. soya protein	10. wasp and bee venom

FASCINATING FACTS ABOUT THE BODY

1. The adult human body is made up of 100 trillion (100,000,000,000,000) cells.
2. A body produces more than $1\frac{1}{2}$ million new blood cells every second.
3. Nerve signals travel around the body at over 200 m.p.h.
4. An average body contains about 10 gallons of water.
5. Every day the body of an average person loses about a half a quart of water—just from breathing.
6. Bones are soft and spongy on the inside.
7. The three tiniest bones in the body are in the ear; together they are about the size of a thumbnail.
8. An ear can distinguish about 400,000 different sounds.
9. A newborn baby has 300 bones; some of them eventually fuse together to form 206 bones in an adult.
10. Nearly half of the bones in the body are in the hands and feet; for example, there are 27 bones in each hand, 5 bones in each palm, and 14 bones in each finger.
11. A few people have been known to lose their second set of teeth and grow a third set.
12. There are over 650 muscles throughout the body—from the tiny ones that move the eyelids to the powerful ones that move the legs.
13. Muscles make up about half the weight of an average body.
14. The most powerful muscle in the human body is the jaw muscle.
15. It takes 72 muscles to speak one word.
16. A child has about 60,000 miles of blood vessels.
17. An average heart pumps about 4,200 gallons of blood every day.
18. It takes blood about 23 seconds to make a complete trip through a body.
19. An average heart beats more than 36 million times a year.
20. On average, a person's skin weighs twice as much as his or her brain.
21. A new layer of skin replaces the old layer approximately every 27 days.
22. Fingernails are made of the same kind of cells as a bull's horns.
23. Nails grow faster in summer than in winter.
24. Fingernails grow 4 times faster than toenails.
25. A newborn baby's brain weighs about 3 ounces, but an average adult's brain weighs about 3 pounds.
26. During an average lifetime, a brain may store up to 100 million bits of information.
27. One out of every 20 people is left-handed.
28. A normal human eye can tell apart about 7 million different shades of color.
29. People have been wearing eyeglasses for more than 700 years.
30. Eyes are constantly in motion—even during sleep.
31. An average nose can recognize up to 1,000 different smells.
32. After you swallow food, it takes about 4 to 8 seconds for it to reach the stomach.
33. The longest record of sneezing without stopping is 155 days.
34. A sneeze can travel at a speed of over 100 m.p.h.
35. An average head contains about 100,000 hairs.
36. Dark hair grows faster than light-colored hair.
37. Each hair on the scalp grows about 5 inches a year.
38. An average person can speak clearly at a rate of up to 300 words per minute.
39. A person with an average appetite will eat more than 35 tons of food in a lifetime.
40. Humans can survive only a few minutes without oxygen, a few days without water, and a few weeks without food.

10 WAYS TO STOP HICCUPS*

1. Hold your breath and then swallow deeply when you feel a hiccup coming.
2. Breath rapidly into a brown paper bag about ten times.
3. Suck on an ice cube or on crushed ice.
4. Chew and swallow a piece of dry bread.
5. Pull your knees up to your chest.
6. Swallow a teaspoon of dry sugar.
7. Suck on a lemon.
8. Rinse your mouth with salt water.
9. Ask someone to tickle you or surprise you.
10. If nothing else works, drink a glass of water while you are upside down, but be careful!

*In 1922, Charles Osborne of Anthon, Iowa, got the worst case of hiccups ever recorded. He hiccuped for 22 years for a total of over 400 million hiccups.

Universe

SOLAR ECLIPSES THROUGH 2000*

Date	Visible in	Kind
1. April 17, 1996	Antarctic	partial
2. Oct. 12, 1996	Arctic	partial
3. March 9, 1997	Russia, Arctic	total
4. Sept. 2, 1997	Antarctic	partial
5. Feb. 26, 1998	Pacific, S. of Panama, Atlantic	total
6. Aug. 22, 1998	Indian Ocean, E. Indies, Pacific	annular**
7. Feb. 16, 1999	Indian Ocean, Australia, Pacific	annular
8. Aug. 11, 1999	Atlantic, England, France, Turkey, India	total

*The first recorded solar eclipse was in China on October 22, 2136 B.C.
**An annular eclipse happens when the moon is too far away to cover the sun completely. As a result, a ring of light appears around the moon.

LUNAR ECLIPSES THROUGH 2000

Date	Type	Midpoint of Eclipse
1. April 4, 1996	total	12:11 a.m.
2. Sept. 27, 1996	total	2:55 a.m.
3. March 24, 1997	partial	4:41 a.m.
4. Sept. 16, 1997	total	6:47 p.m.
5. July 28, 1999	partial	11:34 a.m.
6. Jan. 21, 2000	total	4:45 a.m.
7. July 16, 2000	total	1:57 p.m.

WELL-KNOWN CONSTELLATIONS*

1. Andromeda
2. Aquarius (water bearer)
3. Aries (ram)
4. Cancer (crab)
5. Canis Major (great dog)
6. Canis Minor (little dog)
7. Capricorn (goat)
8. Centaur (centaur)
9. Draco (dragon)
10. Gemini (twins)
11. Leo (lion)
12. Libra (scales)
13. Orion
14. Pisces (fishes)
15. Sagittarius (archer)
16. Scorpio (scorpion)
17. Taurus (bull)
18. Ursa Major (big dipper)
19. Ursa Minor (little dipper)
20. Virgo (virgin)**

*Constellations are patterns of stars. The shapes they seem to make were given names in ancient times; many of those names are still in use today.
**There are 88 recognized constellations.

AN ASTROLOGICAL CALENDAR

Date	Sign	Date	Sign
1. Jan. 20–Feb. 18	Aquarius	7. July 23–Aug. 22	Leo
2. Feb. 19–March 20	Pisces	8. Aug. 23–Sept. 22	Virgo
3. March 21–Apr. 19	Aries	9. Sept. 23–Oct. 22	Libra
4. Apr. 20–May 20	Taurus	10. Oct. 23–Nov. 21	Scorpio
5. May 21–June 20	Gemini	11. Nov. 22–Dec. 21	Sagittarius
6. June 21–July 22	Cancer	12. Dec. 21–Jan. 19	Capricorn

PLANET INFORMATION

	Average Distance From Sun		Average Surface Temperature			
	Mi.*	Km*	F	C	Moons	Rings
1. Mercury	36.0	57.9	332°	167°	0	0
2. Venus	67.2	108.2	854°	457°	0	0
3. Earth	92.9	149.6	59°	15°	1	0
4. Mars	141.7	227.9	-67°	55°	2	0
5. Jupiter	483.8	778.3	-162°	108°	16	1
6. Saturn	887.1	1,427.0	-208°	-133°	18	7
7. Uranus	1,783.9	2,870.0	-344°	-209°	15	11
8. Neptune	2,796.4	4,497.0	-365°	-220°	8	4
9. Pluto	3,666.0	5,900.0	-355°	-215°	1	0

*in millions

LONGEST DAYS ON THE PLANETS

	Length of Day*		
	Days	**Hours**	**Mins.**
1. Venus	244	0	0
2. Mercury	58	14	0
3. Pluto	6	9	0
4. Mars		24	37
5. Earth		23	56
6. Uranus		17	14
7. Neptune		16	7
8. Saturn		10	39
9. Jupiter		9	55

periods of rotation, based on Earth days

LONGEST YEARS OF THE PLANETS

	Length of Year*	
	Years	**Days**
1. Pluto	247	256
2. Neptune	164	298
3. Uranus	84	4
4. Saturn	29	168
5. Jupiter	11	314
6. Mars	1	322
7. Earth		365
8. Venus		255
9. Mercury		88

period of orbit around the sun, in Earth years/days

SPACE AGE FIRSTS

1957   Russia's *Sputnik 1* is the first man-made satellite to orbit the earth.

1957   A Russian dog named Laika is the first animal to go into space. (It died during the flight.)

1960   Two Russian dogs, Strelka and Belka, were the first animals to survive in space on board *Sputnik 5*.

1961   Yuri Gagarin, from Russia, is the first person to orbit the earth.

1962   John Glenn is the first American to orbit the earth.

1962   U.S. *Mariner 2* is the first space probe to reach Venus.

1963   Valentina Tereshkova, from Russia, is the first woman in space.

1969   American Neil Armstrong is the first person to walk on the moon.

1970   The first vehicle on the moon is the unmanned Soviet Lunokhod Rover.

1971   The Russians launch *Salyut 1*, the first space station.

1971   U.S. *Mariner 9* is the first spacecraft to orbit Mars.

1972   *Pioneer 10*, launched by the Americans, is the first space probe sent to the outer planets. (It passed out of this solar system after its mission.)

1973   The U.S. launches *Skylab 1*, its first space station.

1975   A Soviet space probe is the first to transmit pictures from the surface of Venus.

1976   U.S. *Viking* is the first space probe to transmit pictures from the surface of Mars. (No life on Mars is discovered.)

1979   U.S. *Voyager I* discovers that Jupiter, like Saturn, also has rings.

1981   The U.S. sends *Columbia*, its first reusable spacecraft, into orbit.

1983   Sally Ride is the first U.S. woman in space.

1984   Bruce McCandless becomes the first astronaut to fly in space using a self-propelled backpack.

1992   The U.S. *Magellan* space probe successfully completes the mapping of 95% of Venus's surface with radar.

1993   American astronauts repair the Hubble Space Telescope while orbiting the earth.

AN ASTRONOMY TIME LINE

B.C.

2296   Chinese astronomers begin recording the appearance of "hairy stars" (comets)

c. 480   Greek astronomer Oenopides discovers that the earth is tilted.

c. 300   Chinese astronomers compile accurate star maps.

c. 240   Eratosthenes of Greece correctly calculates the size of the earth.

c. 130   Greek astronomer Hipparchus correctly calculates the distance between the earth and the moon.

A.D.

1543   Nicholas Copernicus publishes a book in which he states that the sun, not the earth, is the center of the solar system.

1600   Giordano Bruno is burned at the stake for saying in public that the earth goes around the sun.

1608   Hans Lippershey of Holland invents the telescope.

1610   Galileo observes Jupiter's moons, the phases of Venus, and the rings around Saturn—although he did not know what the rings were at the time.

1668   Sir Isaac Newton makes the first reflecting telescope.

1671   Giovanni Cassini correctly determines the distances of the planets from the sun.

1682   Edmond Halley is the first to describe the comet that is now known by his name.

1781   Astronomer William Herschel discovers the planet Uranus.

1846   Neptune is discovered based on predictions of its position made by John Adams and Urbain Leverrier.

1929   Edwin Hubble finds that the universe is expanding.

1850   The first successful photograph of a star (Vega) is produced.

1930   American astronomer Clyde Tombaugh discovers Pluto.

1963   Quasars are identified for the first time.

1977   The rings around Uranus are discovered.

1986   As predicted, Halley's Comet returns again. *Giotto*, a space probe is able to pass through the comet's tail and send back important information.

1990   The Hubble Space Telescope is launched, but it is soon learned that it has many technical problems, including a misshaped main lens.

1994   Twenty-one fragments of the comet Shoemaker-Levy 9 crash into Jupiter, causing fireballs and long-lasting storms—each the size of the earth—when the fragments hit Jupiter's atmosphere.

Weather and Climate

WEATHER WORDS

Word	Meaning
1. air mass	a large amount of air at a certain temperature and humidity
2. atmospheric pressure	pressure on the earth's surface from the weight of the atmosphere; a rising atmospheric pressure usually predicts calm, clear weather, but falling pressure predicts the opposite, a storm
3. climate	the average weather conditions for a particular area over a long period of time
4. cyclone	a powerful circulating storm with speeds of 73 m.p.h. or more that forms in the Indian Ocean (See *hurricane* and *typhoon* below.)
5. drizzle	liquid water droplets that measure less than 200th of an inch across (See *rain* below.)
6. front	a dividing line between two air masses
7. freezing rain	liquid water that freezes as it hits the ground
8. hail	frozen raindrops that remain in the air because of upward-blowing air currents; water keeps freezing on the surface of the hailstones until they are so heavy that they fall to the ground
9. humidity	the amount of water vapor (water in the form of a gas) in the air
10. hurricane	a powerful circulating storm with speeds of 73 m.p.h. or more that forms in the Atlantic Ocean
11. meteorologist	a person who studies the atmosphere, weather, and weather forecasting
12. monsoon	a system of winds that changes direction between seasons
13. precipitation	the word used for the different forms of water that fall from the clouds—such as rain, snow, and hail
14. rain	liquid water that falls in drops, measuring more than 200th of an inch across
15. sleet	drops of water that freeze in cold air and reach the ground as ice
16. snow	ice crystals that form in the clouds and then fall to the ground
17. thunderstorm	a storm with thunder and lightning
18. tornado	violently circulating winds of more than 200 m.p.h. form a dark funnel that reaches from a cloud down to the ground
19. tropical storm	a circulating storm with wind speeds from 39 to 73 m.p.h.; a tropical storm can develop into a hurricane
20. typhoon	a powerful circulating storm with speeds of 73 m.p.h. or more that forms in the Pacific Ocean

BEAUFORT WIND SCALE*

	Description	Miles Per Hour
0	calm: sea like a mirror	less than 1
1	light air, ripples seen on water	1–3
2	light breeze: wind felt on face	4–6
3	gentle breeze: leaves in constant motion, crests begin to peak	7–10
4	moderate breeze: raises loose paper, small waves become larger	11–16
5	fresh breeze: small trees begin to sway, moderate waves	17–21
6	strong breeze: large branches move, umbrellas used with difficulty, large waves begin to form	22–27
7	moderate gale: whole trees in motion, walking against wind is hard, white foam results from breaking waves	28–33
8	fresh gale: twigs break off trees, wind slows progress, waves grow larger	34–40
9	strong gale: slight structural damage occurs, high waves, tops of waves topple, tumble, and roll over	41–47
10	whole gale: trees uprooted, much damage, very high waves, the sea looks white	48–55
11	storm: very rarely experienced, widespread damage, exceptionally high waves	56–63
12-17	hurricane	64+

The Beaufort Wind Scale was designed in 1805 by Sir Francis Beaufort, a rear admiral in the British navy. His purpose was to describe the wind's effect on sailing ships.

MAJOR TYPE OF CLOUDS

	Description	Prediction	Height*
1. cirrus	thin, feathery	possible rain	4 mi. +
2. cirrocumulus	small patches of white	weather changes	4 mi. +
3. cirrostratus	thin, white sheets	possible rain or snow	4 mi. +
4. stratus	low, gray blanket	rain or snow	0–1 mi.
5. cumulus	flat-bottomed, white puffy	fine weather	1/4–4 mi.
6. cumulonimbus	mountains of heavy, dark clouds	storms	1/4–4 mi.

A ceilometer measures the height of clouds.

WORST VOLCANIC ERUPTIONS IN THE WORLD

	Approx. Number Killed
1. Tambora, Indonesia on April 5-12, 1815	92,000
2. Miyi-Yama, Java in 1793	53,000
3. Mont Pelee, Martinique on May 8, 1902	40,000
4. Krakatoa in Sumatra/Java on Aug. 26-27, 1883	36,380
5. Nevado del Ruiz, Colombia on Nov. 13, 1985	22,940
6. Mount Etna, Italy on March 11, 1669	20,000
7. Laki, Iceland on Jan.-June 1783	20,000
8. Vesuvius, Italy on Aug. 24, 79	16-20,000
9. Vesuvius, Italy on Dec. 16-17, 1631	18,000
10. Mount Etna, Italy in 1169	15,000+

THE RICHTER SCALE* FOR EARTHQUAKES

	Description
1	felt by scientific instruments
2	felt by some people and animals
3	felt by most people
4	felt by all people
5	building walls crack
6	structures tremble
	Major Quake
7	destroys buildings and people
8	a disaster
9	so devastating, none has yet been recorded

Earthquakes throughout the world are measured on this scale, which was created by Charles Richter and Beno Gutenberg, two seismologists.

WORST EARTHQUAKES IN THE WORLD*

	Approx. Number Killed
1. Mediterranean area on May 20, 1202	1,100,000
2. Shenshi, China on Feb. 2, 1556	820,000
3. Calcutta, India on Oct. 11, 1737	300,000
4. Antioch, Syria on May 20, 526	250,000
5. Tang-shan, China on July 28, 1976	242,419
6. Nan-shan, China on May 22, 1927	200,000
7. Yeddo, Japan in 1703 (exact date unknown)	190,000
8. Kansu, China on Dec. 16, 1920	180,000
9. Messina, Italy on Dec. 28, 1908	160,000
10. Tokyo/Yokohama, Japan on Sept. 1, 1923	142,807

In the famous San Francisco earthquake on April 18, 1906, between 500 and 1,000 people died—mostly from the fires that resulted from broken gas pipes and electrical cables following the shock.

COLDEST PLACES IN THE WORLD

	Average Temperatures	
	F	C
1. Norilsk, Russia	12.4 °	-10.9 °
2. Yakutsk, Russia	13.8 °	-10.1 °
3. Yellowknife, Canada	22.3 °	-5.4 °
4. Ulan-Bator, Mongolia	23.9 °	-4.5 °
5. Fairbanks, Alaska	25.9 °	-3.4 °
6. Surgut, Russia	26.4 °	-3.1 °
7. Chita, Russia	27.1 °	-2.7 °
8. Nizhnevartosvsk, Russia	27.3 °	-2.6 °
9. Hailar, Mongolia	27.7 °	-2.4 °
10. Bratsk, Russia	28.0 °	-2.2 °

HOTTEST PLACES IN THE WORLD

	Average Temperatures	
	F	C
1. Djibouti, Djibouti	86.0 °	30.0 °
2. Timbuktu, Mali	84.7 °	29.3 °
3. Tirunelevi, India	84.7 °	29.3 °
4. Tuticorin, India	84.7 °	29.3 °
5. Nellore, India	84.6 °	29.2 °
6. Santa Marta, Colombia	84.6 °	29.2 °
7. Aden, South Yemen	84.0 °	28.9 °
8. Madurai, India	84.0 °	28.9 °
9. Naimey, Niger	84.0 °	28.9 °
10. Hudaydah, North Yemen	83.8 °	28.8 °

COLDEST CITIES IN THE U.S.

	Average Temperatures	
	F	C
1. International Falls, MN	36.4 °	2.4 °
2. Duluth, MN	38.2 °	3.4 °
3. Caribou, ME	38.9 °	3.8 °
4. Marquette, MI	39.2 °	4.0 °
5. Sault Ste. Marie, MI	39.7 °	4.3 °

HOTTEST CITIES IN THE U.S.

	Average Temperatures	
	F	C
1. Key West, FL	77.7 °	25.4 °
2. Miami, FL	75.6 °	24.2 °
3. West Palm Beach, FL	74.6 °	23.7 °
4. Fort Myers, FL	73.9 °	23.3 °
5. Yuma, AZ	73.9 °	23.3 °

Sports Terms • Musical Instruments • The Telephone • Dinosaur Movies • Pet Names
Athletes • Music Composers • Animated Films • Names From Occupations • Sports Term
Musical Instruments • The Telephone • Dinosaur Movies • Pet Names • Athletes • Mus
Composers • Animated Films • Names From Occupations • Sports Terms • Musica
Instruments • The Telephone • Dinosaur Movies • Pet Names • Athletes • Music Composer
Animated Films • Names From Occupations • Sports Terms • Musical Instruments • Th

OUR WORLD

Movies and Television

EARLY ANIMATED FILMS

Film	Stars	Year
1. *Steamboat Willie*	Mickey Mouse, Minnie Mouse, Pegleg Pete	1928
2. *The Chain Gang*	Pluto	1930
3. *The Little Wise Hen*	Donald Duck	1934
4. *Donald Duck*	Donald Duck, Daisy Duck	1937
5. *Snow White and the Seven Dwarfs*	Snow White, Bashful, Doc, Dopey, Grumpy, Happy, Sleepy, Sneezy,	1937
6. *Fantasia*	Mickey Mouse, Apollo, Ben Ali Gator, Mademoiselle Upanova, Yensid	1940
7. *Pinocchio*	Pinocchio, Figaro, Gepetto, Jiminy Cricket, Monstro, Stromboll	1940
8. *Dumbo*	Dumbo	1941
9. *Bambi*	Bambi, Bambi's Mother, Ant Ena, Thumper	1942
10. *Song of the South*	Blynken, Br'er Bear, Br'er Rabbit, Mr. Bluebird, Tar Baby	1946

DINOSAUR MOVIES

Movie	Year
1. *King Kong*	1933
2. *Fantasia*	1940
3. *Journey to the Center of the Earth*	1959
4. *One Million Years B.C.*	1966
5. *When Dinosaurs Ruled the Earth*	1970
6. *One of Our Dinosaurs Is Missing*	1975
7. *At the Earth's Core*	1976
8. *Baby . . . Secret of the Lost Legend*	1985
9. *The Land Before Time* (animated)	1988
10. *Jurassic Park*	1993

FAVORITE MOVIES OF YOUNG PEOPLE*

1. Jurassic Park
2. The Lion King
3. E.T.—The Extra Terrestrial
4. 101 Dalmatians
5. Star Wars
6. Fantasia
7. The Jungle Book
8. Aladdin
9. Home Alone
10. Ghostbusters
11. Back to the Future
12. Beauty and the Beast
13. Raiders of the Lost Ark
14. Three Men and a Baby
15. Return of the Jedi
16. Home Alone II: Lost in New York
17. Batman
18. The Empire Strikes Back
19. Pinocchio
20. Who Framed Roger Rabbit?
21. Teenage Mutant Ninja Turtles
22. Bambi
23. Big
24. Terminator 2: Judgment Day
25. The Terminator
26. Cocoon
27. Close Encounters of the Third Kind
28. Honey, I Shrunk the Kids
29. The Wizard of Oz
30. Look Who's Talking

*Based on box office sales and purchases and rentals of videos up until 1995.

FILMMAKING TERMS

Term	Meaning
1. close-up	a picture that is taken near the subject
2. director	the person who decides how the filming and acting should be done
3. dolly	a moving carriage that carries the camera
4. dubbing	the process of adding sound to a film
5. freeze	a shot that is held so that the action seems to stop
6. flashback	an interruption in the story of a film to recall a past event
7. long shot	a shot taken from a distance
8. pan	short for *panoramic short*, a sideways sweep by the camera
9. producer	the person responsible for the general making of a film, apartfrom the directing
10. prop	short for *property*, an object used by an actor—such as a book
11. rushes	the day's shots before editing
12. scenario	the scene-by-scene outline of a film script
13. shooting	filming a scene
14. storyboard	a drawing like a cartoon strip that shows the exact sequence of a particular scene
15. take	part of a scene that is shot without any interruption

A TV TIME LINE

1930 Philo T. Farnsworth develops the cathode-ray tube, which becomes the basis of the modern viewing screen.

1930 Vladimir Zworykin develops the image orthicon tube, which becomes the basis of the television camera.

1930 RCA opens WZRBX, an experimental TV station in NY on July 30.

1934 Congress establishes the Federal Communication Commission (FCC) to regulate the broadcast industry.

1936 The British Broadcasting Company begins its first public television broadcasting service.

1938 NBC televises live news for the first time.

1939 NBC begins its first regular television broadcast service in the U.S.

1939 Franklin Roosevelt becomes the first president to appear on television.

1939 CBS and Dumont networks begin programming, but World War II slows development.

1941 The FCC grants its first commercial TV licenses to NBC and CBS on July 1 in New York.

1945 The FCC assigns 13 channels for commercial broadcasting in the U.S.

1946 Television begins to replace radio as the leading communications industry.

1946 Philadelphia, PA, and Schenectady, NY, receive programs from NBC in New York

1947 The World Series is broadcast on TV for the first time. (The NY Yankees beat the Brooklyn Dodgers in 7 games.)

1949 The National Academy of Television Arts and Sciences presents its first Emmy Awards for TV programs.

1951 Fifteen million TV sets are in operation—up from only 1.5 million a year before.

1951 The first transcontinental TV broadcast is made.

1952 The *Today Show* begins on NBC.

1954 RCA markets the first electronic color televisions that met FCC standards.

1955 Dwight Eisenhower is the first President to have his news conference aired on TV.

Music

SOME GREAT COMPOSERS

Name	Major Accomplishments
1. Johann Sebastian Bach (German: 1685–1750)	His major works can be divided into three areas: organ works, instrumental and orchestral works, and religious choral works. He is best known for the *Brandenburg Concertos*, the *Goldberg Variations*, and *The Well-Tempered Clavier*.
2. Ludwig van Beethoven (German: 1770–1827)	His symphonies, overtures, concertos, piano sonatas, and string quartets are considered some of the world's greatest. He is particularly famous for his nine symphonies.
3. Johannes Brahms (German: 1833–1897)	He wrote masterpieces in almost every form except opera. He is most famous for his four symphonies and rich piano music.
4. Frédéric Chopin (Polish: 1810–1849)	His expressive music established the piano as a solo instrument. His music has become the most frequently played piano music in history.
5. George Gershwin (American: 1898–1937)	His combination of American styles (jazz and blues) with impressionist harmony was a major influence on 20th century American music. He is best known for *Rhapsody in Blue, An American in Paris*, and the opera *Porgy and Bess*.
6. George Frideric Handel (German: 1685–1759)	He composed Italian operas, oratorios, and many instrumental pieces. Today he is most famous for *The Messiah*.
7. Franz Joseph Haydn (Austrian: 1732–1809)	His development of the sonata-symphony form and style earned him the title of "Father of the Symphony."
8. Wolfgang Amadeus Mozart (Austrian: 1756–1791)	No other composer before or after him could ever compete with him for speed and ease of composition. In his short life, he produced over 600 works. Two of his most famous operas, which are often heard today, are *The Magic Flute* and *Don Giovanni*.
9. Igor Stravinsky (Russian-American: 1882–1971)	He is widely considered the most influential composer of the 20th century. He is most famous for his ballets *Petrushka, The Firebird*, and *The Rite of Spring*.
10. Peter Ilyich Tchaikovsky (Russian: 1840–1893)	He is considered the most popular 19th century composer for his melodic flair and vivid orchestration. He is best known for his ballets, symphonies, the *1812 Overture*, and the *First Piano Concerto*.

TYPICAL INSTRUMENTS OF A 100-PIECE ORCHESTRA

1. string section

32 violins	10 cellos	1 harp
12 violas	8 basses	

2. woodwind section

1 piccolo	4 bassoons	3 oboes
3 flutes	4 clarinets	

3. brass section

3 trumpets	5 French horns	3 trombones
1 tuba		

4. percussion section
   (pitched)

timpani (kettledrums)	xylophone
glockenspiel (bells)	chimes

   (unpitched)

bass drum	gong
snare drum	triangle
cymbals	woodblocks

NATIVE INSTRUMENTS FROM AROUND THE WORLD

Instrument	Country
1. alpenhorn	Switzerland
2. bagpipe	Scotland
3. balalaika	Russia
4. cimbalon	Hungary
5. gusla	former Yugoslavia
6. marimba	Guatemala
7. sitar	India
8. spike fiddle	Thailand
9. steel drums	West Indies
10. trompong	Bali

A TIME LINE OF THE RECORDING INDUSTRY

1877   Thomas Edison records "Mary Had a Little Lamb" on November 20th on a tinfoil cylinder. Those are the first sounds ever recorded.

1888   German-born American inventor Emile Berliner invents the Gramophone, a recording on a flat disc. His patent is purchased by the Victor Talking Machine Co.

1888   Josef Hoffman, a 12-year-old pianist, makes the first recording at the Edison Laboratories in New Jersey.

1892   First "Berliner" records are sold, marking the first mass production of music on records.

1903   *Vesti la Biubba* by Italian tenor Enrico Caruso becomes the first record to sell one million copies.

1903   Nicole Freres makes the first unbreakable record out of cardboard covered with shellac.

1915	Records at 78 rotations per minute (RPM) replace the cylinders. (Each side lasts about $4\frac{1}{2}$ minutes.)
1919	Radio Corporation of America (RCA) is founded.
1925	Researchers at Bell Laboratories invent the first successful electric phonograph.
1927	The Victor Talking Machine Company of New Jersey introduces the first record changer.
c. 1930	Coin-operated jukeboxes become very popular.
1940	*Billboard* publishes the first pop record sales chart.
1940	Walt Disney's movie *Fantasia* is the first movie to use stereophonic sound.
1948	CBS Laboratories produce the long-playing (LP) record. (Each side records from 5 to 20 minutes.)
1949	RCA makes the first small 45-rpm record. (At this time there were now 16 million record players in use.)
1951	Deutsche Gramophone markets the first 33-rpm LP record. (In the U.S., about 190 million records are sold this year.)
1952	American Bandstand televises its first show.
1953	"Crazy Man Crazy," a song by Bill Haley and His Comets is the first rock 'n roll song to make the *Billboard* charts.
1954	Musician Les Paul builds the first multitrack (8-track) tape recorder.
1954	George Eash, a Los Angeles engineer, invents tape cartridges.
1957	Stereo technique for recording two-channel sound in a single groove is perfected.
1958	Stereo LPs are marketed for the first time in the U.S.
1959	The National Academy of Recording Arts and Sciences presents its first Grammy Awards.
1963	The Beatles, the best selling musical group of all time, releases "She Loves You," their first U.S. single. (Total record sales by the Beatles are estimated at more than 1 billion as of 1985.)
1969	Over 500,000 people attend the first Woodstock Music Festival in upstate New York.
1970s	American electrical engineer Thomas Stockholm, Jr., invents the compact disc (CD).
1981	Music Television (MTV) premieres on cable network.
1989	Digital audio tape recorders, which can compete with the quality of compact discs, are marketed in the U.S. for the first time.

MOST POPULAR GIRLS' AND BOYS' NAMES*

Girls' Names	Boy's Names
1. Brittany	Michael
2. Ashley	Christopher
3. Jessica	Matthew
4. Amanda	Joshua
5. Sarah	Andrew
6. Megan	James
7. Caitlin	John
8. Samantha	Nicholas
9. Stephanie	Justin
10. Katherine	David

*In the 1990s.

MOST POPULAR SURNAMES IN THE U.S.

1. Smith
2. Johnson
3. Williams/Williamson
4. Brown
5. Jones
6. Miller
7. Davis
8. Martin/Martinez/Martinson
9. Anderson/Andersen
10. Wilson

NAMES FROM OCCUPATIONS*

Last Name/Occupation

1. Barker/shepherd
2. Black/dyer
3. Chamberlain/personal servant
4. Chandler/candlemaker
5. Cooper/barrelmaker
6. Leach/doctor
7. Parker/park keeper
8. Smith/metal worker
9. Stone/stone worker
10. Wall/mason

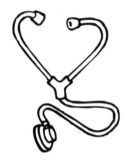

*In 12th-century England when family names began to be used, people were often called by what they did. For example, if a baker were named John, he became John Baker.

MOST ASKED ABOUT HISTORICAL PEOPLE*

1. John F. Kennedy (1917-1963), U.S. President
2. William Shakespeare (1564-1616), English playwright and poet
3. Sigmund Freud (1856-1939), Austrian founder of psychoanalysis
4. Ernest Hemingway (1894-1961), U.S. novelist and journalist
5. Martin Luther King, Jr. (1929-1968), U.S. civil rights leader and clergyman
6. Robert Frost (1874-1963), U.S. poet
7. Edgar Allan Poe (1809-1849), U.S. poet and short story writer
8. Mark Twain [Samuel Clemens] (1835-1910) U.S. novelist
9. Charles Dickens (1812-1870), English novelist
10. Emily Dickinson (1830-1886), U.S. poet
11. John Steinbeck (1902-1968), U.S. writer and novelist
12. Leonardo da Vinci (1452-1519), Italian painter, sculptor, and engineer
13. Al Capone (1899-1947), U.S. gangster
14. John Locke (1632-1704), English philosopher
15. Herman Melville (1819-1891), U.S. novelist

The Encyclopedia Britannica's Instant Research Service answers more than 170,000 questions a year. More questions are asked about these people than any others.

FAMOUS LEFT-HANDED PEOPLE

1. Alexander the Great
2. Larry Bird
3. Napolean Bonaparte
4. George Bush
5. Lewis Carroll
6. Bill Clinton
7. Kurt Cobain
8. Ty Cobb
9. Natalie Cole
10. Tom Cruise
11. Leonardo da Vinci
12. Albert Einstein
13. Ben Franklin
14. Lou Gehrig
15. Keith Hernandez
16. Reggie Jackson
17. Caroline Kennedy
18. Marcel Marceau
19. Harpo Marx
20. Michelangelo
21. Paul McCartney
22. Marilyn Monroe
23. Luke Perry
24. Shanna Reed
25. Babe Ruth
26. Norman Schwarzkopf
27. Jerry Seinfeld
28. Ringo Starr
29. Queen Victoria
30. Oprah Winfrey

Musical Instruments • The Telephone • Dinosaur Movies • Pet Names • Athletes • Mu
omposers • Animated Films • Names From Occupations • Sports Terms • Music

MOST POPULAR PETS IN THE U.S.*

Percent of homes

1. dogs   36.5%
2. cats   30.9
3. birds   5.7
4. fish   2.8
5. horses   2.8
6. rabbits   1.5
7. hamsters 1.0
8. guinea pigs 0.5
9. gerbils   0.3
10. ferrets 0.2

Cats are actually more popular than dogs because people who own cats usually have more than one per house. As a result, people own approximately 52,500,00 dogs and 57,000,000 cats.

MOST POPULAR NAMES FOR DOGS AND CATS

Dogs

1. Brandy
2. Lady
3. Mad
4. Rocky
5. Sam
6. Heidi
7. Sheba
8. Ginger
9. Muffin
10. Bear
11. Misty
12. Duke
13. Pepper
14. Princess
15. Coco
16. Prince
17. Charlie
18. Daisy
19. Buddy
20. Buffy

Cats

1. Kitty
2. Smokey
3. Shadow
4. Tiger
5. Boo/Boo Boo
6. Boots
7. Molly
8. Tigger
9. Spike
10. Princess
11. Patches
12. Sam
13. Max
14. Mickey
15. Samantha
16. Whiskers
17. Fluffy
18. Katie
19. Blackie
20. Coco

MOST COMMON DOG TRICKS

1. sit
2. shake a paw
3. roll over
4. "speak"
5. lie down
6. stand on hind legs
7. beg
8. dance
9. "sing"
10. fetch the newspaper

Sports

SPORTS TERMS

Baseball	Basketball	Football	Ice Hockey	Soccer	Others
at bat	air ball	block	assist	chip	alley
base hit	backboard	down	face-off	dribble	Axel
bunt	basket	fair catch	goalie	free kick	birdie
diamond	charging	gridiron	hat trick	kickoff	bogey
fly	court	huddle	high-sticking	match	chip
foul	dribble	kickoff	icing	offside	gait
glove	free throw	offside	offside	pass	love
homer	guard	pass	pass	pitch	mogul
inning	hoop	punt	power-play goal	rebound	parry
mitt	jump shot	quarter	puck	save	putt
pitch	key	safety	shorthanded goal	screen	rack
strike	rebound	tackle	Stanley Cup	tackle	schuss
walk	slam dunk	touchdown	stick	throw-in	telemark

OLYMPIC SPORTS*

Summer Sports

1. archery
2. bobsleding
3. baseball
4. basketball
5. boxing
6. canoe/kayaking
7. cycling
8. diving
9. equestrian**
10. fencing
11. field hockey
12. football (soccer)
13. gymnastics
14. rhythmic gymnastics
15. judo
16. modern pentathlon***
17. rowing
18. shooting
19. softball
20. swimming
21. synchronized swimming
22. table tennis
23. team handball
24. tennis
25. track and field
26. volleyball
27. water polo
28. weight lifting
29. wrestling
30. yachting

Winter Sports

1. biathlon****
2. bobsled
3. ice hockey
4. luge (toboggan)
5. figure skating
6. speed skating
7. Alpine skiing
8. freestyle skiing
9. Nordic skiing*****

*The 2000 Olympic Summer Games will be held in Sydney, Australia . The 1998 Winter Games will be held in Nagano, Japan, and the 2002 Winter Games in Salt Lake City, Utah.
**Equestrian, a 3-day event, includes dressage and show jumping.
***Modern pentathlon, a 5-day event, includes cross-country running, riding, fencing, pistol shooting, and swimming.
****Biathlon includes cross-country skiing and rifle marksmanship.
*****Nordic skiing combines Nordic and Alpine styles.

OLYMPIC FIRSTS

1896 The first modern Olympic Games are held in Athens, Greece.

1900 Women compete in the Olympic Games for the first time; six women participate in lawn tennis.

1908 For the first time, medals are awarded to the first three people to finish each event.

1920 The Olympic flag, the Flight of Doves, is raised for the first time, and the Olympic oath is introduced.

1924 The Winter Olympics are held for the first time in Amsterdam.

1928 The Olympic flame is introduced.

1936 The first games are televised.

1984 ABC broadcast 200 hours of Olympic events over two weeks.

1994 Starting in 1994, the Winter Olympic Games are held two years after the Summer Olympics—rather than in the same year.

SPECIAL OLYMPICS EVENTS*

Summer Sports

1. aquatics
2. athletics (track and field)
3. basketball
4. bowling
5. cycling
6. equestrian
7. gymnastics
8. roller skating
9. soccer
10. tennis
11. volleyball

Demonstration Sports

1. badminton
2. golf
3. polo hockey (like floor hockey)
4. powerlifting
5. table tennis
6. team handball

Winter Sports

1. Alpine skiing
2. cross-country skiing
3. figure skating
4. floor hockey
5. speed skating

*The International Special Olympic Games, athletic competition for mentally retarded people 8 years old and up, are held every four years. For more information, write to Special Olympics International Headquarters, 1350 New York Ave. N.W., Washington, D.C. 20005.

NOTABLE FEATS OF YOUNG ATHLETES

Name (age)	Accomplishment
1. Deborah Wilson (11)	She became the youngest member the 111 Mountain Climbing Club ever had. To qualify, she had to climb 111 mountains in the U.S. Northeast. She was 5 when she climbed her first 4,000-foot mountain.
2. Kirsen Wilhelm (9)	In 1977, he became the youngest American to ride a bicycle across the U.S. The trip took him 66 days.
3. Richard Daff Jr. (11)	He was the youngest bowler to score a perfect 300 game.
4. Karen Stead (11)	She was the first girl to win the All-American Soap Box Derby.
5. Joe Nuxhall (15)	In 1944, he became the youngest baseball player to play on a major league team, the Cincinnati Reds.
6. Tai Babilonia (12) Randy Gardner (14)	In 1974, these two young people became the youngest ice skaters to represent the U.S. in international competition.
7. Boris Becker (17)	He was the youngest tennis player to win at Wimbledon.
8. Nadia Comaneci (15)	In the 1976 Olympics, she was the first to earn a perfect score of 10 in a gymnastic event. She also won 3 gold medals in gymnastics that same year.
9. Anne Lewis (10)	In 1968, she became the youngest rodeo star, winning a world title in barrel racing.
10. Coby Orr (5)	He was the youngest golfer ever to shoot a hole-in-one. He hit the ball 103 yards, which is 3 yards longer than the length of a football field.
11. Tracy Austin (16)	In 1979, she became the youngest champion in the history of the U.S. Open Tennis Championship.
12. Frank Wooten (9)	He became the youngest jockey to win a race.
13. Jorge Lebron (14)	In 1974, he became the youngest basketball player ever to be signed as a rookie by a major league team, the Philadelphia Phillies.
14. Margaret Castro (17)	In 1977, she became the youngest woman to win an international Grand Championship in judo.
15. Frederick Garcia (8-months)	Although he couldn't walk yet, he became the youngest person ever to pass the Red Cross water safety beginner's test.

MOST POPULAR SPORTS-RELATED ACTIVITIES IN THE U.S.*

Activity	Participants	Activity	Participants
1. walking	70,800,000	6. camping	42,900,000
2. swimming	60,300,000	7. bowling	37,400,000
3. bicycle riding	49,800,000	8. billiards/pool	34,000,000
4. fishing	45,700,000	9. basketball	28,200,000
5. exercising with equipment	43,800,000	10. motor/power boating	26,400,000

*According to the National Sporting Goods Assoc., only 18,100,000 Americans play softball, and only 15,100,000 play baseball.

SPORTS' HALLS OF FAME

	Mailing Address
1. International Boxing Hall of Fame	P.O. Box 425 Canastota, NY 13032
2. Naismith Memorial Basketball Hall of Fame	P.O. Box 179 1150 West Columbus Ave. Springfield, MA 01101
3. National Baseball Hall of Fame	P.O. Box 590 Cooperstown, NY 13326
4. National Football Foundation and Hall of Fame	Bell Tower Building 1865 Palmer Ave. Larchmont, NY 10538
5. National Tennis Foundation and Hall of Fame	100 Park Ave. New York, NY 10017

FAVORITE SPORTS AROUND THE WORLD*

Sport	Especially Popular In
1. badminton	India, Malaysia, Thailand
2. baseball	Caribbean Islands, Japan, U.S.
3. basketball	Italy, Mexico, Russia, U.S.
4. bicycle riding	France, Italy, Germany
5. bobsledding	Germany, Switzerland
6. boccie (lawn bowling)	Italy
7. golf	Great Britain, U.S.
8. gymnastics	China, Japan, Russia, U.S.
9. hockey, field	India, Pakistan, Germany
10. hockey, ice	Canada, Finland, Russia, Sweden, U.S.
11. hurling	Ireland

12. judo	Japan, South Korea
13. polo	Argentina, Australia, Great Britain, India
14. rowing	Canada, Great Britain, U.S.
15. skiing, Alpine	Italy, Sweden, Switzerland
16. skiing, Nordic	Finland, Norway, Sweden
17. swimming	Australia, Germany, U.S.
18. table tennis	China, Japan
19. tennis	Australia, Great Britain, Sweden, U.S.
20. volleyball	China, Russia, U.S.

Soccer, known as football in most parts of the world except Canada and the U.S., is the most popular sport in the entire world.

Things

RED LETTER DAYS: THEIR ORIGINS

Holiday (year)	Background
April Fool's Day	April 1st used to be known as the French New Year's Day. After the Gregorian calendar was adopted, it became known as a "fool's holiday" after those who refused to change their celebration from April 1st to January 1st. It became a time to give silly gifts and play jokes.
Arbor Day (1872)	First celebrated in Nebraska as a day for planting trees.
Christmas (342)	Christmas was first celebrated on December 25th as a Christian holiday.
Easter (325)	Emperor Constantine proclaimed that Easter, celebrating Christ's resurrection, would be celebrated on the first Sunday after the full moon on or after the vernal equinox.
Father's Day (1910)	Father's Day was first celebrated in Spokane, Washington. Then in 1972, President Richard Nixon proclaimed Father's Day an official national holiday.
Groundhog Day (c. 1550)	This tradition began in Germany where farmers believed a legend about a badger forecasting the coming of spring. Nineteenth century immigrants to the U.S. switched to a groundhog and chose February 2nd as the official date.
Hanukkah (165 B.C.)	First celebrated in Palestine, Hanukkah honors the Jewish victory in the Maccabean revolt against the Syrians.
Halloween (c. 400 B.C.)	The Festival of Samhain on October 31st was first observed by the ancient Celts in Ireland. Bonfires celebrated the summer's harvest and were thought to frighten away evil spirits. It later became known as Halloween.

Independence Day (1777)	The first Independence Day was celebrated on July 4th with the ringing of church bells, fireworks, bonfires, and music.
Martin Luther King Day (1983)	This holiday, in memory of the slain civil-rights leader, gained national acceptance 15 years after his death.
Mother's Day (1908)	Known earlier in Europe, Mother's Day was first celebrated in West Virginia. By 1911, all U.S. states recognized the holiday.
New Year's Day (1582)	Christians moved the New Year holiday to January 1 when the Gregorian calendar was adopted. It replaced a medieval celebration that lasted from March 25 to April 1.
St. Patrick's Day (432)	This religious holiday honored the arrival of St. Patrick in Ireland. St. Patrick's Day was first celebrated in the U.S. in 1737 by a Protestant group that organized to help homeless and unemployed Irishmen.
St. Valentine's Day (313)	To encourage Romans to convert, Christians adopted several holidays. During this one, young men drew the names of eligible women from a box. The earliest known Valentine was sent in 1415 from Charles, Duke of Orleans, to his wife during his imprisonment in the Tower of London.
Thanksgiving (1621)	Colonists in Plymouth, Massachusetts, joined with American Indians in November to celebrate their first successful harvest. Later it became known as Thanksgiving. Then in 1789, President George Washington first proclaimed Thanksgiving Day (then on November 26th) as a national holiday in order to give thanks for the Constitution. However, political opposition blocked its acceptance until 1863 when President Abraham Lincoln made Thanksgiving a national holiday.
Veterans' Day (1954)	November 11th was proclaimed a holiday in honor of all those who fought for the nation. It replaced Armistice Day, which was a celebration to mark the end of World War I.

EVERYDAY THINGS: WHEN THEY FIRST APPEARED

c. 1490	The toothbrush is invented in China, but toothbrushes with nylon bristles are not sold until 1938.
1810	The tin can is patented in England but does not become commercially popular until 1865.
1845	Rubber bands are patented in Great Britain.
1848	The first Yale locks are invented by Linus Yale in the U.S.
1872	The first square-bottom grocery bag is invented in the U.S.
1879	Edison demonstrates the first light bulb.
1887	Contact lenses are developed.
1888	The ballpoint pen makes its first appearance.

1888	Kodak markets its first home camera.
1889	Aspirin is introduced in Germany but does reach the U.S. until 1915.
1893	Zippers are demonstrated at the World's Columbian Exposition in Chicago.
1900	The paper clip is patented.
1908	Disposable paper cups make their first appearance.
1915	Lipstick is marketed for the first time.
1920	Home radios are introduced.
c. 1920	Johnson & Johnson produces its first Band-Aids.
1924	Disposable handkerchiefs appear on the market.
1928	Adhesive tape is available for the first time.
1930	The first pop-up toaster is marketed.
1937	Cellophane tape, known as "Sellotape," can be purchased.
c. 1954	Color television is marketed for the first time.
1955	Inexpensive transistor radios go on sale.
1960	Felt-tipped pens are marketed successfully.
1963	The first home video recorders become available.
1963	Push-button phones are new on the market.
1970	The first videocassette recorder (VCR) especially designed for home use is introduced.
1970s	Compact-disc (CD) technology becomes available.
1974	Electronic pocket calculators are sold for the first time.
1975	Sales of the first desktop microcomputer are great.
1979	Consumers see their first Sony Walkman.
1989	Household plastic wrap in various colors becomes available.

POPULAR KIDS' COLLECTIONS

1. action figures
2. animal figures
3. Barbie dolls
4. baseball cards
5. bookmarks
6. books
7. bottle caps
8. CDs/cassette tapes
9. comic books
10. dolls/doll houses
11. video games
12. gum wrappers
13. horse figurines
14. Hot Wheels cars
15. keys
16. marbles
17. Matchbox cars
18. miniatures
19. models
20. movies on video
21. paper dolls
22. postcards
23. posters
24. rocks
25. seashells
26. stamps
27. stickers
28. Teddy bears
29. troll dolls
30. famous people's autographs

20TH CENTURY FADS

1901	Americans first discover ping-pong.
1902	Owner of a store in Brooklyn, New York, sells the first "teddy bear," named after U.S. President Theodore Roosevelt.
c. 1909	Jigsaw puzzles become very popular.
1924	Marathons become popular; for example, an ex-sailor sits on the top of a flagpole for over 13 hours.
1926	Two New York businessmen promote the first game of miniature golf.
1933	Out-of-work man in New Jersey creates Monopoly.
1939	Goldfish swallowing becomes popular on college campuses.
1939	Rollerskate dancing attracts hundreds of young people.
c. 1940	"Zoot suits" with big padded shoulders and baggy pants are the rage.
1945	Silly putty is developed but only marketed as a toy four years later.
1946	Bikini bathing suits first appear in Europe.
1947	Bubble-gum-blowing contests become popular.
1952	Over 30 million children wore propeller-topped hats.
1955	Pizza becomes a favorite food for almost everyone.
1957	A game using the Frisbee becomes a recognized sport.
1958	The first Barbie doll is manufactured.
1958	The hula hoop, which may be the biggest fad in history, is introduced.
1959	College students stuff themselves into telephone booths.
1960	Americans now own 85 million tv sets.
1961	FCC chairman Newton Minow says that American television programming is a "vast wasteland."
1961	The yo-yo, which was first introduced in 1929, becomes an instant fad.
1962	The first Americans get addicted to video games.
1963	Television becomes the main source of news for Americans.
1964	Products related to the Beatles take in $50 million in one year.
1964	Satellite television, which is demonstrated for the first time, makes worldwide broadcasting possible.
1968	News program *60 Minutes* begins.
1969	Over 100 million people throughout the world watch the first American astronauts land and walk on the moon.
1970	Cigarette ads are banned from television and radio.
1970	CDs (compact discs) get off to a slow start.
1975	Pet Rocks are sold everywhere.
1975	Skateboarding sweeps across the country.
1980	Cable television, with about 4,225 channels, is becoming popular.
1981	MTV (music television) makes its first broadcast in the U.S.

1982	The National Institute of Mental Health announces that violent TV programming is harmful to viewer.
1982	Japan is the first country to offer wristwatch televisions.
1983	Cabbage Patch dolls become an overnight sensation.
1986	Fox becomes the fourth major TV network.
1989	Teenage Mutant Ninja Turtles begin a new craze among the young.
1990	Rollerblading is taken up by the athletic and energetic.
1994	Power Rangers are watched and imitated by children everywhere.

THE TELEPHONE: ITS HISTORY

1876	Alexander Graham Bell patents his telephone, a one-piece transmitter-receiver.
1878	The first telephone switchboard begins operation in New Haven, Connecticut.
1878	Long-distance calls are made possible by the development of Thomas Edison's carbon-type microphone telephone transmitter.
1887	U.S. telephone companies now serve 150,000 customers.
1892	The first automatic switchboard is used.
1893	Boston and Chicago are linked for the first time by long distance telephone.
1900	Telephones with a separate earpiece and mouthpiece are introduced.
1905	Dial telephones are developed but not put into use immediately.
1915	Vacuum tubes make cross-country and trans-Atlantic calls possible.
1921	First completely automatic local dialing service is offered in Omaha, Nebraska.
1926	First trans-Atlantic conversation is made between New York and London.
1947	Microwave relay stations, which replace expensive trunk lines, create long distance communication between Boston and New York.
1950	Black rotary dial phones are introduced.
1951	Direct long distance dialing service begins in the U.S.
1956	Visual telephones are developed in the U.S.
1962	The world's first telecommunications satellite, called *Telstar*, is put into orbit.
1963	Push-button phones are offered for the first time.
1966	For the first time people can make direct-dial calls to Europe.
1970	First commercial Picturephone service begins in Pittsburgh, Pennsylvania.
1985	Single optical fibers, which carry as many as 300,000 calls at once, are created at Bell Laboratories.

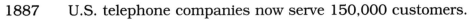